THE WOLVES AND MOOSE
OF ISLE ROYALE

THE WOLVES AND MOOSE
OF ISLE ROYALE

Restoring an Island Ecosystem

Text by **NANCY F. CASTALDO**   Photographs by **MORGAN HEIM**

CLARION BOOKS
An Imprint of HarperCollinsPublishers

For my husband, Dean, and researchers Rolf and Candy Peterson —NFC

For my mother, Dorothy Gehgan, who instilled my love for nature at an early age, and always encouraged me to pursue my dreams. —MH

Clarion Books is an imprint of HarperCollins Publishers.

The Wolves and Moose of Isle Royale
Text copyright © 2022 by Nancy F. Castaldo
Photographs copyright © 2022 by Morgan Heim

ISBN: 978-0-35-827423-0

Photo Credits:
All photos taken by Morgan Heim, with these exceptions: NPS/Lindsey Welch: p. iv, USFWS/Ryan Hagerty: p. 2;
NPS: pp. 3, 4, 38, 42, 44, 45, 54; Nancy F. Castaldo: pp. 7, 8, 10, 12, 14, 17, 19 (second from top), 24 (top), 40, 66 (left), 75, 84;
NASA Satellite Image: map p. 4; David Mech: p. 27; NPS/Rolf Peterson: p. 28-29; NPS/Paul Brown: p. 31;
NPS (Yosemite Archives, Joseph Dixon Collection): p. 34; NPS/Jacob W. Frank: p. 36, 43 (right); UWFWS/Courtney Celley: p. 39;
NPS/Michael Runtz: p. 41; NPS/John Pepin: p. 43 (left); NPS/Jim Peaco: p. 46; NPS/Kaitlyn Knick: p. 59; NPS/Yeva Cifor: p. 84

Typography by Cara Llewellyn
22 23 24 25 26 RTLO 10 9 8 7 6 5 4 3 2 1

First Edition

CONTENTS

THE ARCHIPELAGO OF ISLE ROYALE

RISING OUT OF THE COLD, deep waters of Lake Superior are a group of islands, miles from any shoreline. These isolated islands form Isle Royale National Park, the least visited of all the United States' sixty-three national parks, but one of the parks with the most returning visitors. Here, a drama is unfolding between two animals: wolves (*Canis lupis*) and moose (*Alces americanus*).

In the midst of the island's seclusion and serenity, the relationship between these two species has fascinated scientists all over the world for more than fifty years, creating the longest **predator/ prey** study in history. Even schoolkids as far away as Norway learn about the important role wolves play on this island. I studied it, too, in my college ecology class.

Wolves, often maligned and hunted throughout history, help keep today's Isle Royale **ecosystem** in balance as predators of the island's ever-munching **herbivores**, or plant eaters, moose.

In the case of the Isle Royale ecosystem, wolves are foundational to the health of this particular island environment. They help the entire ecosystem remain stable so that it doesn't topple like a disproportioned tower of cards. Moose are also important to the island, as they fill the roles of both prey and herbivore. As their numbers grow, so does their impact on the balance of the ecosystem. These large herbivores strip the island of vegetation, like the

MOOSE

Alces americanus
Mammal, cervid, herbivore

WEIGHT: On average 1,000 pounds
HEIGHT: Over 6 feet (1.8 m) tall on average
LENGTH: 8–11 feet (2–3 m)
Males grow antlers up to 6 feet (1.8 m) across
AVERAGE LIFESPAN IN THE WILD: 8–12 years
STATUS: Species of special concern in Michigan
FUN FACT: Moose comes from an Algonquin name meaning "eater of twigs."

WHAT IS AN ECOSYSTEM?

An ecosystem is an environmental community consisting of all the organisms living in a particular physical area that function together as a unit. It includes plants, animals, micro-organisms, soil, and even the rocks, minerals, and water. It's like a classroom filled with students, a teacher, desks, and everything else that is part of a schoolroom. Sometimes an ecosystem can get off-balance with too much of one part or too little of another part.

Have you ever made a tower of cards? Each card is important to the structure. If you pull out any load-bearing cards, the tower will collapse. Now, picture your tower with an overabundance of cards on the top layer, making it ready to topple. Or imagine your classroom with too many students, making it crowded, especially if there aren't enough desks for everyone! It's the same with any ecosystem.

saplings of quaking aspen (*Populus tremuloides*), yellow birch (*Betula alleghaniensis*), and balsam fir (*Abies balsamea*). In areas where moose have eaten a lot of plants, scientists have found changes in the soil chemistry that impact the availability of nitrogen for plant growth. The moose's heavy trampling of the land can also change its configuration, as their large hooves create spaces in the earth along with the destruction of plants. Even island wetland habitats are impacted. In all, moose alter the forest/vegetation community on the island and the entire ecosystem. Although moose play an important role in the ecosystem, too many of them cause the tower to wobble.

The National Park map shows the location of Isle Royale in Lake Superior, as well as trails, and access points by boat and seaplane.

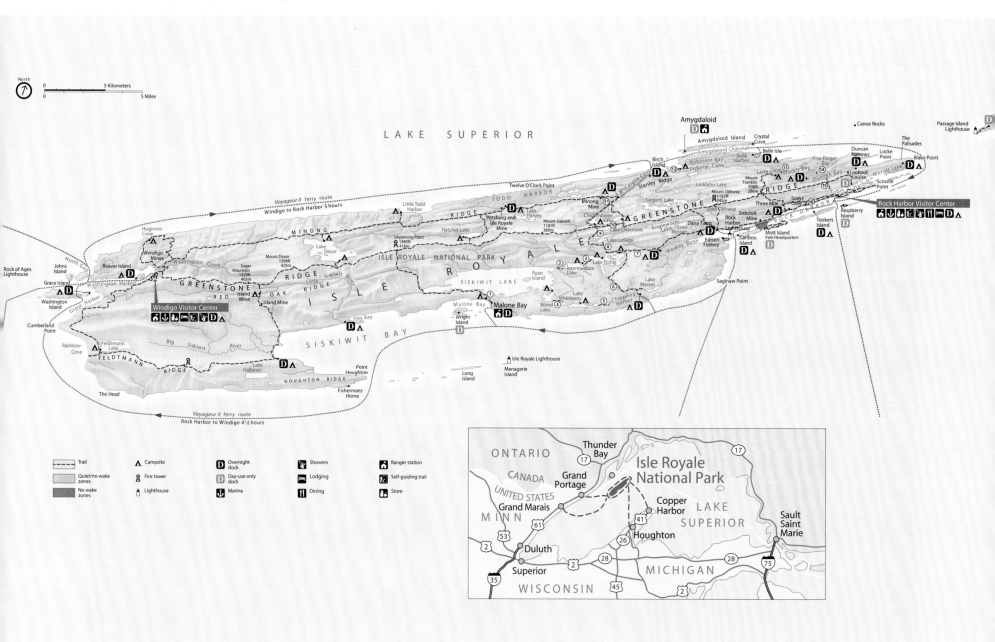

With the number of wolves on the island having dropped and the number of moose increasing, the Isle Royale ecosystem is in jeopardy—and scientists are taking drastic measures to restore the balance. They've decided to bring in wild wolves from the mainland through a controversial reintroduction process called genetic rescue.

It's time to head to Isle Royale National Park and see this reintroduction experiment firsthand.

ISOLATED ISLAND

THE ISOLATION OF THIS NATIONAL park, an **archipelago** of over 450 islands in Lake Superior (the largest of which is Isle Royale), has created an intriguing stage for the wolf-moose drama. But its remote location—two hundred and seventy-eight miles (447 km) from Ontario, Canada, forty miles (64 km) from Grand Portage, Minnesota, and sixty-one miles (98 km) from Houghton, Michigan—makes researching this "living laboratory" challenging for scientists, according to moose researcher Dr. Rolf Peterson. It also makes this national park an exception for visitors who might be used to vacationing at parks with a variety of accommodations and dining. Isle Royale is too far away from the mainland to have a bridge, so you can't pack your family into a car and drive to it. It has one lodge, several rustic cottages, camping shelters accessible only to hikers, and numerous camping sites. It is limited to one small restaurant in Rock Harbor, serving guests until seven p.m. each night. Cell service is nonexistent, and Wi-Fi minimally available. In addition, the park completely shuts down for over six months each year due to its inaccessibility during the colder months, when the boats stop sailing.

As hard as the island is to reach for humans, it's also challenging for animals. Because of its distance in Lake Superior, only a mere nineteen native mammal species, compared to over forty found on the nearest mainland, have been able to access the island and establish populations. There is also a special mixture of plants that thrive there, including

species not found elsewhere in that region.

Isle Royale's unique mix of plants and animals living in such an isolated location has made it all the more exciting for scientific research. The island's serenity and beauty, combined with its scientific fascination, makes it well worth the trip for any visitor. I wanted to see it all for myself and share it with you, so photographer Morgan Heim and I set off to meet researchers and explore.

THE ADVENTURE BEGINS

THE ONLY WAY TO REACH this island research site in the Great Lakes is by seaplane or boat. Morgan and I choose to board the National Park Service's 165-foot (50-km) *Ranger III*, which travels between Houghton, Michigan, and Isle Royale's Rock Harbor. Since the ship leaves on just a few mornings this early in June, we fly into the small, one-gate airport of Hancock in Michigan's Upper Peninsula (UP) the day before. We stay near the launch site in Houghton, enjoying the small UP lakeside village and a fish dinner caught fresh from Lake Superior.

The next day we head out to the dock on the largest of America's Great Lakes and also the largest body of fresh water on the planet. Lake Superior can be dangerous and has a rich history of shipwrecks. Choppy waters or fog can cause sailings to be canceled or delayed. But not today. The sun is shining, and the lake is clear.

Boarding begins for the seventy-three-mile (117-km) boat journey, which will take between five

The US National Park Service *Ranger III*, sailing out of Houghton, Michigan, is the largest of four vessels that transport park visitors and researchers to Isle Royale.

Before boarding the *Ranger III*, all passengers must swipe their shoes to clean off any seeds or unwanted pests that might find their way to the island ecosystem.

and six hours. A careful swipe of our shoe bottoms over the cleaning brushes before walking up the gangplank prevents any uninvited pests or seeds that would upset the balance of Isle Royale's natural ecosystem—especially during a time when researchers are working hard to restore it.

The whistle blows, and we're off, sailing past the lighthouse into open water. Even in the summer, hypothermia is a real danger in the cold waters of this lake, so we need to take extra safety measures. The crew teaches us about putting on a special protective flotation suit, called a Gumby, in case we find ourselves overboard. This full-body suit will protect us better than a standard life jacket by helping us stay warm. We look at each other. This definitely highlights one of the risks of visiting the park.

Since we don't see land for hours, it feels as if we're in open sea. The lake is more ocean-like than lake-like, with views of shimmering, white-capped water stretching into the horizon. We settle in and enjoy the Park Service videos that jump-start our island research.

A ROCKY START

THE ISLAND'S HISTORY BEGAN WITH its creation, long before its human occupation. The earth's crust was ripped open a billion years ago. Lava flowed out and hardened into a slab of basalt rock. Over millions of years, that process of rock formation happened again and again. It created a giant layer cake of rock. That rocky stockpile cracked, shifted, and tilted.

Later, glaciers scraped across the earth, the thick sheets of ice carving furrows in the softer rock. When the last major glacial retreat occurred around eleven thousand years ago, a pattern of ridges and valleys formed.

Melting ice was trapped in a deep basin around the rock layers, creating Lake Superior, one of the five Great Lakes. But we can still see the result of that rocky heap that shifted and pitched. It's Isle Royale. The forty-five-mile-long (72-km-long) island of tilted rocks pokes up out of that deep lake, which, for comparison, is roughly the size of the state of Rhode Island.

People began to inhabit this isolated island in the cold, dark waters of Lake Superior 4,500 years ago. We know this from evidence left behind—copper diggings, bits of pottery, and the bones of fish, caribou, and beaver that exhibit scars from

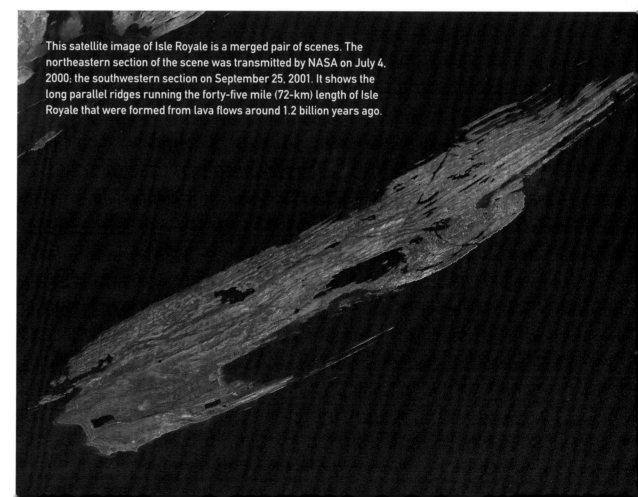

This satellite image of Isle Royale is a merged pair of scenes. The northeastern section of the scene was transmitted by NASA on July 4, 2000; the southwestern section on September 25, 2001. It shows the long parallel ridges running the forty-five mile (72-km) length of Isle Royale that were formed from lava flows around 1.2 billion years ago.

Shaft holes of copper mines give hikers a chance to discover the early human history of the park. There were nine mining companies on the island between 1843 and 1893.

tools and human teeth. The archaeological record shows us that the earliest human inhabitants were using copper for tools, ornaments, and spearheads, as did some of their possible descendants, the Grand Portage Ojibwa. They called the island Minong, meaning "good high place," and enjoyed it for copper mining, hunting, and fishing. The Grand Portage Band (Gichi-Onigaming) were the traditional users of Minong. Today, park visitors are reminded of this early island name as they visit Minong Ridge and the challenging Minong Trail.

Although French missionaries renamed the island Isle Royale, meaning "royal island" in the 1600s, European settlers didn't begin to reside on the island for another two hundred years.

In those early years of habitation by Americans of European descent, the island also attracted loggers, lighthouse keepers, fishers, and homesteaders.

These early American settlers appropriated the island and its resources from native populations and encouraged more European-Americans to come.

During this period of early settlement, the Anishinaabeg nations along Lake Superior shores in Wisconsin and Minnesota, including the Grand Portage Band, signed land treaties (1842 and 1844) with the US government for Minong.

More than half a century later, scientists became intrigued by the island. In the summer of 1905, six scientists from the University of Michigan, led by Dr. Charles Adams, landed at Isle Royale's round brick Rock Harbor Lighthouse. Although the 1859 lighthouse was closed in 1879, they set up their camp on the site. The research team included experts in all different wildlife species. For the next month, they studied everything from birds to beetles on Isle Royale. Dr. Charles Adams's final ecological report, *An Ecological Survey of Isle Royale*, set the model for future research. It demonstrated how to collect field data and analyze it at a time when the study of ecology was brand-new. The report not only spurred more field study but also laid the groundwork for scientists' enduring fascination with the island.

This historic lighthouse is one of the first structures we spotted on Isle Royale from the deck of the *Ranger III*.

Noted American travel writer T. Morris Longstreth wrote about the appropriateness of Isle Royale's name in 1924, in his book *The Lake Superior Country*: "This shard of a continent becalmed in the green fresh-water sea is indeed royal, isolate, and supreme." Summer cabins, fishing camps, and hotels sprang up during the 1890s through the early 1920s. More and more people found their way to the shores, including a conservation columnist for the *Detroit News* named Albert Stoll.

He played a role in the island's designation as a national park through writing about it after his September 1921 visit. The residents had formed the Citizens' Committee of Isle Royale to help preserve the island as a park. Stoll became their spokesperson and key advocate. In 1924, he organized a trip to Isle Royale that included influential people, like Stephen Mather, the first director of the National Park Service, and Hubert Work, the secretary of the interior. Stoll's voice—and that of the island's remaining residents—was heard.

Isle Royale was declared a national park on April 3, 1940, and was officially dedicated in 1946, after World War II. Most of the residents sold their homes and their islands to the government, though some were then given lifetime leases, allowing them to rent and continue to live on that land. Other residents weren't given money for their land at all, because the government considered them squatters rather than owners. Today a few life leaseholders,

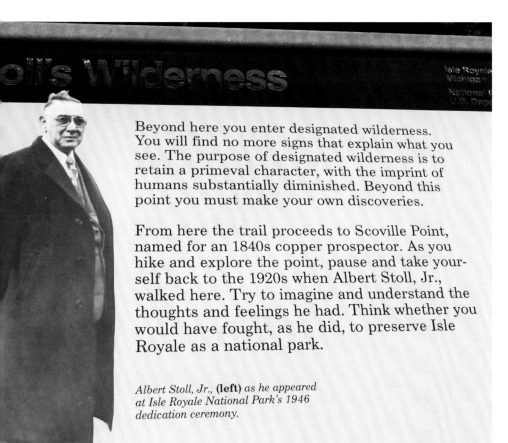

oll's Wilderness

Isle Royale
Michigan

National
U.S. Dep

Beyond here you enter designated wilderness. You will find no more signs that explain what you see. The purpose of designated wilderness is to retain a primeval character, with the imprint of humans substantially diminished. Beyond this point you must make your own discoveries.

From here the trail proceeds to Scoville Point, named for an 1840s copper prospector. As you hike and explore the point, pause and take yourself back to the 1920s when Albert Stoll, Jr., walked here. Try to imagine and understand the thoughts and feelings he had. Think whether you would have fought, as he did, to preserve Isle Royale as a national park.

Albert Stoll, Jr., **(left)** *as he appeared at Isle Royale National Park's 1946 dedication ceremony.*

Trail signs mark the place where Albert Stoll Jr. walked in the 1920s and ask hikers to imagine why he was inspired to preserve the land.

whose families originally owned island properties, are left. They continue to carry on the island traditions of vacationing, berry picking, fishing, and gathering together.

But humans weren't the only migrants to the islands. While people were using the islands throughout history, animals also found their way there.

MOOSE AND WOLVES ARRIVE

WHEN THE EARLIEST WOLVES CROSSED over to the "supreme" island around 1949 on natural ice bridges that regularly formed during winters on the frozen lake between the island and the mainland, the moose were already there. No one knows exactly how the moose arrived. Most scientists believe that the moose also crossed from the mainland over the ice bridges to the archipelago.

But Tim Cochrane, former Grand Portage

National Monument superintendent, offered another possibility in a 2013 paper. He suggested that moose were captured live on the mainland and shipped to the island around 1900—though that is unproven. No matter how they arrived, they settled in. Without a natural predator, their population faced various ups and downs. The moose population grew to over a thousand. Then their numbers crashed in 1934 as food became scarce and moose unhealthier.

Although Isle Royale wolves prey on other creatures, like snowshoe hare (*Lepus americanus*) and beaver (*Castor canadensis*), their main diet is moose.

Wolves are a vital **keystone species** in the island ecosystem. A keystone species is like the main ingredient in a big chocolate cake. The recipe wouldn't work without the chocolate. Keystone species keep the rest of the ecosystem healthy. They are vital. Wolves are the chocolate. On Isle Royale, the wolves keep the moose population healthy and their numbers in check by preying on the weak and old of the herd. Unlike most human hunters, who often strive to kill the strongest and biggest animals, wolves prey on the vulnerable, leaving the strongest individuals to breed. This hunting strategy helps the entire moose herd. But if the numbers of wolves and moose grow lopsided, the island ecosystem becomes threatened.

A healthy ecosystem can support a finite number of moose, or any species for that matter. That number is known as the **carrying capacity**. If that number is exceeded, the ecosystem becomes unhealthy.

That is the case on Isle Royale now. The island ecosystem is off-balance. There are too few wolves and too many moose. In early 2018, there were only two wolves left on the island and around two thousand moose. A healthier ratio would be nineteen wolves to about nine hundred moose.

Because of this imbalance, the forest landscape is not regenerating. The centuries-old balsam trees that form the canopy on the island are reaching the end of their life. They are responsible for seeding the island with new growth. The shorter, younger trees on the island face the ever-expanding herd of munching moose. Few seedlings are living to maturity.

This impacts the source of food for moose and causes them to suffer from starvation. The herd is becoming less healthy. Other species are also affected. That is why scientists are working to restore the balance by bringing wolves to the island.

ISLAND LABORATORY OR CIRCUS?

Isle Royale's predator/prey study is the oldest on the planet. Founded by scientist Durward Allen in 1958, it is formally called the Isle Royale Wolf-Moose Study. The study was a joint project between Purdue University and the National Park Service, under the support and direction of park naturalist Bob Linn.

Allen viewed the island as a living laboratory, which he defined as a place "where the animals you are counting and studying do not wander away."

Dr. Rolf Peterson took over the project twelve years after it began. He had the experience of having studied wolves and moose in Alaska. Since the 1970s, he has agreed with Allen and claimed that the island's isolation created an "ideal natural laboratory." The Isle Royale study "is more important than other studies where humans have a greater impact on the natural world. Isle Royale is unusual because nature runs wild where animals and trees are not harvested by humans," he claims, whereas "on the mainland you have people shooting moose and abusing wolves nonstop."

Several island ecosystems, the Galapagos included, have also been viewed as living laboratories.

While the criteria Durward Allen described are met on Isle Royale, Rolf Peterson's wife, Candy Peterson, voices a different opinion. Calling the island a laboratory makes her, as a nonscientist, feel somewhat excluded. Candy says, "a laboratory excludes the general public, for whom the parks were established." And, Candy adds, "labs are for tinkering, and the island is a natural park, a look-see sort of place; tinkering is not allowed." She's right. Even if a moose is discovered stuck in the mud, researchers allow nature to take its course and only observe. But if the island isn't a "laboratory," what is it? Candy sees the island as "a huge circus with the animals in charge."

Can you picture the island as a circus, with us as spectators, watching and observing their goings-on?

LAND AHOY!

LAND! WE SAIL PAST THE Isle Royale lighthouse before stopping at Mott Island, one of the park's many smaller islands, to drop off supplies for Isle Royale National Park rangers and researchers. The ship docks beside a variety of smaller National Park research boats. We disembark and enjoy a few moments on land before boarding the ship again for the short journey to our final stop. Meanwhile,

ABOVE LEFT: The sign on Mott Island, home of Isle Royale's park headquarters, welcomes visitors to the national park.
ABOVE: The stop at Mott Island gives everyone a chance to disembark while supplies are delivered to the park's rangers and researchers.

the cargo doors open on the *Ranger III*. Cartons of latex gloves, fresh eggs, beverages, peanut butter, and other provisions for living and working on the island are loaded onto rolling carts, forming a train of supplies pulled by a John Deere tractor for eager National Park employees and researchers.

After reboarding, we soon dock at Rock Harbor, our final destination. The six-hour voyage is completed. We are finally on Isle Royale proper, the largest island and namesake of the national park.

This is where we'll stay for the week. One by one, we join campers and explorers making their way down the gangplank. Except for the water lapping against the wooden dock, sand, and rocks, it's noticeably quiet. No car sounds or taxis honking. No hustle and bustle. The island is so far out into

The small, quiet Rock Harbor plays host to the large *Ranger III,* as well as small crafts, like national park research vessels.

the lake that sounds generate only from the island itself: bird calls, wind, and gentle waves rising against the shore. June sunlight warms our faces as cool breezes blowing off the chilly lake make us glad for the extra layer of clothing we've added.

Morgan and I settle into the lodge and hit the trails that begin right outside our lakeside rooms. We climb from the shoreline toward the Greenstone Ridge, which runs like a spine along the island, and soon notice the change in our surroundings.

Lichens, combinations of two types of organisms (algae and fungi), hang from the trees in the boreal forest ecosystem. Today they can warn scientists about air quality. Researchers have found that moderate levels of sulfur have reached the island's lichens via the air.

It's rare at this early time in the season to see anyone else on the island's trails.

Boreal, or northern, forest with cold-tolerant spruc-
es draped in old man's beard moss, balsam fir, and
paper birch surround us. As we hike inland, away
from the cool waters and breezes, it gets warmer.
We can unzip our jackets and shed a layer. The tree
species also change. Sugar maples and red oaks
poke up from the rocky ground.

Among the sunshine-yellow marsh marigolds
that line the wetter areas of the trails and the
sparks of tiny purple orchids that draw our eye,
there are also plants that shouldn't be naturally
this far south or east. Northern paintbrush, with
its spiky white flower, and orchid-like three-toothed
saxifrage have found their way south to these
shores. It's believed the seeds of these plants were
deposited here from the Arctic during the last ice
sheet retreat. Imagine a big snowball moving down
a hill, picking up stuff along the way, but also de-
positing things that fall off—that's what happened
with the ice that moved across that area. The seeds
were in the ice, and as it moved across the land, the
seeds became freed from the ice and were left behind to grow. There's also the thimbleberry, a tasty

Two of the island's 600 flowering plants are marsh marigolds
(top two photos) and calypso orchids (bottom two photos).

treat for wildlife and people, usually only found west of the Rocky Mountains.

We keep our eyes peeled for Isle Royale's cast of supporting characters, including snowshoe hare, red squirrels, fox, beaver, bats, and others, which have created subplots in the main drama between wolves and moose over the last several decades.

It's exciting to visit the island in early June, when the days are long and we're able to hike well after ten p.m. In the morning, we'll start meeting the research team.

Snowshoe hare might resemble your local cottontail, but they have much larger feet and different coloring that helps them survive in their colder surroundings.

THE TEAM

THE ISLE ROYALE RESEARCH TEAM is multifaceted. There are staff who maintain the health of the entire island system, headed up by the Isle Royale National Park superintendent. There are also scientists who conduct long-term moose and wolf research on behalf of the national park, the United States Forest Service, and universities. In addition, support staff arrive each summer in varying capacities. They help on specific projects, work as interns, and serve as field associates.

One of the specific projects many of them are involved with during our visit is the wolf reintroduction project planned to repair the ecosystem's balance. It involves bringing wolves from the mainland to strengthen the island's wolf population and increase the population's genetic diversity. The hope is that the new diversity will not only further the number of wolves on the island and control the moose population, but also create healthy, strong packs that will survive into the future. As an added benefit, it will enable the world's longest predator/prey study to continue, providing additional information for scientists.

Morgan and I are here to learn from the team. Let's meet them.

DR. ROLF PETERSON—MICHIGAN TECHNOLOGICAL UNIVERSITY PROFESSOR AND ECOLOGIST

Rolf Peterson

Dr. Rolf Peterson was just nine years old when Durward Allen began the Isle Royale Wolf-Moose Study. He later took over the study when Allen retired, in 1975, and has been in charge ever since. He and his wife, Candy, live on the island each summer. They coordinate a group of volunteers, called Moosewatch, who collect moose bones on the island throughout the summer to help in the long-term study of the moose population behaviors and health on the island. Rolf is also involved in the wolf reintroduction project and tracking the island's live moose.

CANDY (CAROLYN) PETERSON—EDUCATOR AND FIELD ASSISTANT

Candy Peterson

Candy has assisted with the moose study with Rolf for over four decades. She is the heart of the Moosewatch program, providing food for the visiting researchers and welcome information to all park visitors who stop by Bangsund Cabin, where she and her husband live and work each season. Over the years, she has also served as a field assistant and logistics expert.

PHYLLIS GREEN—ISLE ROYALE NATIONAL PARK SUPERINTENDENT

Phyllis Green

For eighteen out of her forty-one years of federal service, Phyllis Green has been at Isle Royale. Her role at the 571,790-acre (2,314-km^2) park is to supervise all activities, including our visit. Over her career she has worked on and led programs to combat invasive aquatic species in Lake Superior, bring sustainable solar power to the park, upgrade visitor facilities, plan historic wilderness preservation activities, and deal with the issues the island ecosystem has faced related to the dwindling wolf population. We are lucky to be able to work with Phyllis on our visit just before her retirement.

MARK ROMANSKI—CHIEF OF NATURAL RESOURCES

As chief of natural resources for Isle Royale National Park, biologist Mark Romanski oversees much of the wolf-moose study and the recent reintroduction of wolves to the island. He grew up on a river, fishing and hunting, but dreamed of a career in marine science. That dream changed after coming to Isle Royale as a volunteer during college, working and studying under Rolf Peterson. He transitioned to wildlife biology and has been full-time since 1996.

Mark Romanski

project to reintroduce wolves to the island in an effort to rewild, or restore, the damaged ecosystem to a more natural, healthy state. Lynette was involved in the release of the first wild wolves in 2018.

Lynette Potvin

He lives on Mott Island from May to September each year.

LYNETTE POTVIN—US FOREST SERVICE ECOLOGIST

Ecologist Lynette Potvin has worked for the United States Forest Service for three years. She first came to Isle Royale while still in high school. Her brother worked for Rolf, and she helped him collar wolves after college. She now has a master of science in forest ecology and concentrates on studying the island's vegetation, while still being involved in the

CARA RATTERMAN—WILDLIFE TECHNICIAN

As a wildlife technician, Auburn University graduate Cara Ratterman spends her days investigating the wolf population of the island under the direction of Mark Romanski. She takes the information generated from the wolf collars to explore how and

COLLARING WILDLIFE

There are many ways for scientists to monitor animals in the wild. Whether it is a collar that fits around the neck of an animal or a tag that attaches to an ear or a wing, each contains a mechanism, like GPS, that sends signals back to researchers with vital data. Among the data, scientists can see where individual animals are and how long they stay in that location.

While all of the wolves that are being introduced to Isle Royale are tagged and collared, park scientists are also attempting to "smart" collar as many moose as they can. Smart collars provide all sorts of info, such as external temperature and GPS location, and even include an accelerometer that can detect movement, similar to a Fitbit or smart watch for humans. It's through this monitoring that wildlife technicians and interns, like Cara and Izzy, can conduct their observations.

Ecologist Mark Romanski holds up a wolf collar used to help researchers track the island's wolves.

Wildlife tags fastened to the ears of released wolves, similar to human earrings, assist researchers in monitoring wolves on the island.

where they are living on the island. Cara spends her days and nights in the field, hiking to study sites and returning valuable data to the teams of scientists.

Cara Ratterman

IZZY (ISABELLA) EVAVOLD—SEASONAL BALSAM FIR INTERN

University of Montana student Izzy Evavold has one year left to finish her undergraduate degree in wildlife biology. This summer, she's a seasonal balsam fir intern, studying that species throughout the park, but she is also engaged in using **telemetry** to locate newly collared moose that feed on her subject. Telemetry enables Izzy to receive the radio signals sent out from nearby collared moose. She then uses those signals to move closer and observe their behavior. Since moose eat balsam, Izzy gets to study the trees and the moose during her island internship.

Isabella (Izzy) Evavold

Morgan Heim

NANCY CASTALDO—AUTHOR

And then there's me, Nancy Castaldo. I've been studying the environment and writing about our planet and its inhabitants for decades, including America's endangered wolf populations. Like many predators, wolves are often seen as a threat, but that can be a misconception in the larger scheme of our natural environment. My fascination with wolves began when I studied Rolf's work in my college ecology class—making this research trip even more exciting. And while I've visited my share of national parks, this is my first visit to Isle Royale.

MORGAN HEIM—PHOTOGRAPHER

Morgan is on board as the photographer of this book. She's a senior fellow with the International League of Conservation Photographers and a former North American Nature Photography Association board member. Morgan's photographed a lot of wildlife, including the migration of mule deer across Wyoming, endangered birds in China, and bison recovery in the American Plains. Like mine, this is her first visit to Isle Royale.

Nancy Castaldo

AN ISLAND OUT OF BALANCE

THE ISLE ROYALE FASCINATION PARTY began before I was born. The first Isle Royale wolves that caught the world's attention—and Rolf Peterson's—were described in an early 1960s article by Durward Allen and L. David Mech in the popular *National Geographic* magazine. A research aircraft captured a striking image of a wolf pack chasing down moose on Isle Royale. With fifteen wolves, it became known as the Big Pack.

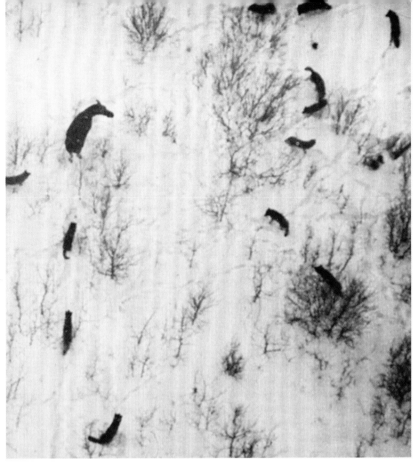

This 1960s photo by Isle Royale researcher L. David Mech shows wolves holding moose at bay.

The island's wolf population peaked around 1980, when there were fifty wolves on the island and 664 moose observed through the annual Winter Study, which has been going on for over sixty years. These annual observations still continue through the use of a plane flying above the island.

Wolves keep moose herds healthy by preying on weak and injured moose, allowing the strong to survive and breed. When the moose population is lower and the individuals are strong, the island also remains healthy. Moose require about forty pounds (18 kg) of vegetation per day to survive. That is a lot of plant munching for an island with a growing moose population. In contrast, you might have deer living near you. White-tailed deer are small, distant cousins on the moose family tree. They don't live on Isle Royale now, but they do live on the mainland, where they eat only around nine or so pounds (4 kg) of vegetation a day. That's a big difference. Hungry moose can change a forest quickly.

As the moose population has had ups and downs, so have the numbers of wolves. The wolf population took a drastic dive in 1982—shrinking from five packs to two, or fifty wolves to fourteen—due to many human factors, including the introduction of parvo, a canine disease, believed to have been brought to the island by a domestic dog. The disease spread to the wolves, making them fatally sick. This reduction in predators allowed for the moose population to grow unchecked. Dogs are not allowed on the island now unless they get special permission and have extensive veterinary clearances to prevent this from happening again.

Imagine a country farm with a number of cats that control the mice or rat population. If the cats were suddenly removed, the barn would get overrun with rodents looking for an easy meal. It's similar on the island with moose and wolves.

With the decline of wolves, the moose population rose to 700 that year. The following year, the number of wolves increased to twenty-three, but the increase wasn't enough to keep the moose

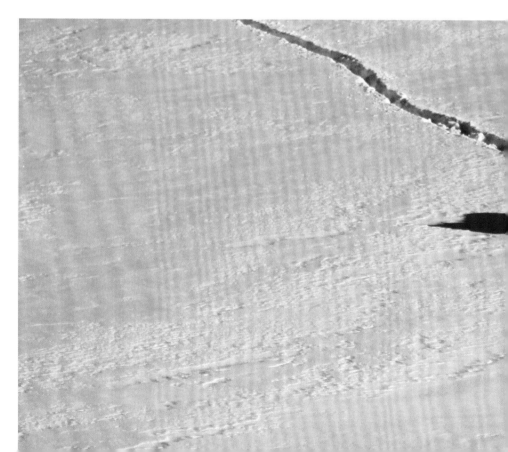

numbers at bay. Their numbers rose to 900. From 2007 to 2017, the moose population tripled to about 1,600.

The numbers of moose and wolves fluctuated for years, increasing the imbalance, until only two wolves, a father and daughter, remained, and the number of moose rose to over two thousand. These last two wolves, a nonbreeding, bonded pair, were probably immune to the ravaging parvo disease that killed the others. But they could not keep the growing moose population healthy. And since they were not having young, the wolf population would die with them if no other wolves came to the island.

And even that was unlikely. The father-daughter duo appeared to be very territorial of their island habitat, as noted by researchers who witnessed occasional wolves coming naturally to the island and leaving shortly after. Researchers recorded three wolves crossing the ice in 2018, but they left after checking out the island and probably encountering the unwelcoming native father-daughter pair.

Another factor in the declining wolf population: the rising temperature of Lake Superior's waters. It has increased more than the air temperature, creating a 70 percent decline in the formation of the ice bridges that were crucial to the island's wolf population. The lack of naturally forming ice bridges has prevented other wolves from regularly reaching the island from the mainland. This, in turn, contributes to the lack of genetic diversity of the wolves, which would strengthen the wolf population.

There are other changes too. Mark Romanski, Isle Royale's chief of natural resources, tells me that the weather played a significant role in the wolf

Two wolves are spotted from above, crossing the ice.

decline: "There are more winds and more waves." Mark notes that these erratic weather conditions have dramatically increased. The **polar vortex**, which refers to winds from the cold arctic, is occurring more frequently. A warmer lake brings more snow to the island, but higher winds prevent ice from forming, decreasing the opportunities for bridges to the mainland. There is also more rain in the fall and, later, greater snowfall accumulation to trudge through, which impacts the entire ecosystem, making travel, hunting, and food foraging more difficult for wolves.

While these weather patterns continue to impact the island's wolves, they also affect the quality of life for the moose population. With a lack of predation, the number of moose has been growing. This has caused food to become scarce, as greater numbers of moose browse on the island's finite vegetation. This overbrowsing behavior prevents forest regeneration.

As a result, moose have been dying of starvation. They have suffered not only from starvation but also from illness, and high winter tick loads caused

Hungry moose strip the bark from trees.

by the warming weather weaken them. By 2007, the tick levels were so high that at the end of that year, most moose had lost roughly 75 percent of their hair from tick infestation.

The **boreal forest** itself also suffers, as balsam

An ever-growing, hungry moose population leads moose to suffer from starvation. This moose carcass, though, will help researchers learn about the health of the population.

trees die off and spruce trees and grasses become more prevalent. Without forest regeneration, the ecosystem will topple. For example, the lack of new balsam growth further contributes to the stress on the ecosystem, as seen in the changing populations of other island animal species. The numbers of ravens and fox have also decreased, with fewer dead animals to provide them with scavenging opportunities. Without many predators, the snowshoe hare population rose in number about five years ago, but vegetation overgrazing and climate change took their toll, and their numbers then plummeted.

Something needed to be done to restore the island's balance—and fast; otherwise, the Isle Royale that researchers and visitors knew, studied, and loved would be irrevocably changed.

The endangerment of the native animal and plant population, and the island's inability to course-correct without human interference (ironically the same reason why Isle Royale faced these issues in the first place), led to much discussion and debate among scientists, the public, and the National Park Service.

WHY NOT JUST HUNT THE MOOSE?

If there are too many moose, why not just hunt them? In September 2019, after the mainland wolves were reintroduced to Isle Royale, Michigan lawmakers proposed a resolution (H.R. 0154) in the Michigan House of Representatives to allow moose hunting in the national park in the midst of the ongoing wolf reintroduction project. Park managers had decided against a hunt a few years earlier when discussing the possibility of reintroducing wolves to Isle Royale.

Still, lawmakers argued, "You're talking about a once-in-a-lifetime opportunity to go on a moose hunt," said Michigan Republican Representative Steven Johnson. "It's really a win-win-win."

And even if hunting were allowed on Isle Royale, the 134,000-acre (540-km²) wilderness has no roads, making the logistics of removing a large moose carcass near impossible. Hunters would face challenges on the island from the lack of roads to transport their kill to the lack of ways to preserve it in such a remote location. To hold a moose hunt during spring, fall, or winter would be improbable in the changeable weather on the isolated island.

"You're out on an island in the middle of Lake Superior with no refrigeration. A whole moose would weigh half a ton," said Rolf Peterson.

Representative Johnson knew that rangers had secured moose meat to supply newly transplanted wolves with an easy meal upon their release, and he used this knowledge to argue that allowing hunters access to the island was the same thing. But that meat was harvested previously, not hunted for the release. It was designed to keep the introduced wolves and the ecosystem healthy.

The debate continued, with Johnson defending human hunters over a pack of wolves. He insisted that human hunters are "more humane than a pack of animals taking down a moose."

But there is a one crucial difference. Human game and trophy hunters often strive to kill the strongest, biggest animal they can. Wolves search out the weak, diseased, old, or frail. Wolves leave the healthy moose in the herd, enabling strong genes to pass to another generation. This natural predator-prey relationship is visible in the behavior both species exhibit in the wild. For example, when a wolf attacks a healthy moose, the moose stands its ground. The wolf backs away. If the moose is ill, lame, or weak, it runs, and the wolf joins in fast pursuit. What do you think happens when a strong, healthy moose stands its ground when approached by a human hunter?

In addition, the uniqueness of Isle Royale is partially due to the fact that neither wildlife nor woodland are harvested by humans. Areas like this are rare in the world and have contributed to the island's importance to researchers.

Although it will take time to establish new wolf packs on Isle Royale, park scientists are surely up to the task of keeping the moose population and the island ecosystem healthy.

DEBATING WOLF REINTRODUCTION

WHAT WERE THE DIFFERING OPINIONS on reintroducing wolves to the island? As with any big decision, there were those in favor and those opposed. Those who opposed the reintroduction focused their argument on a few main issues. They believed that the island should not be tampered with in any way. This centered on the 1964 Wilderness Act's definition of *wilderness*. It states that a wilderness is "an area where the earth and its community of life are untrampled by man, where man himself is a visitor who does not remain . . . an area of undeveloped Federal land retaining its primeval character and influence, without permanent improvements or human habitation, which is protected and managed so as to preserve its natural conditions . . ." A key point in this policy focused on nonintervention. If Isle Royale is defined as a wilderness, how could researchers intervene by reintroducing a species?

Others opposed the plan because they believed that wolves and moose were "exotic" creatures who had come from elsewhere and didn't belong on the island in the first place. Perhaps researchers should let the populations go extinct, or "wink out."

Another viewpoint offered the possibility of introducing a former resident predator/prey relationship to the island featuring two different animals—lynx and caribou. Before the island became a national park, Canada lynx (*Lynx canaensis*) and woodland caribou (*Rangifer tarandus caribou*) lived on Isle Royale. They were **extirpated**, meaning removed from this region by humans. Lynx were trapped. Caribou were extirpated by the settlers who hunted them and who had also removed their food source—the red and white pine. The last caribou was seen in 1925 on Isle Royale, and lynx were gone by the 1930s. Some wondered if the island should be restored to that period. After all, caribou are rarer than moose.

In 2011, Indiana University professor Philip Scarpino prepared a paper for the National Park Service focused on balancing human and natural

Before wolves and moose made their marks on the island, woodland caribou, like this one, called the island home.

history in the park. He referred to both moose and wolves as "exotic" species but also called them iconic species, important symbols of the park's wildness that have helped define Isle Royale National Park. He also questioned what is "natural" on Isle Royale in the context of wilderness. More points to consider.

Months later, three researchers from Isle Royale, Michigan Tech University ecologist John Vucetich, Michigan State environmental philosopher Michael Nelson, and researcher Dr. Rolf Peterson, laid out their thoughts in a paper titled, "Should Isle Royale Wolves Be Introduced? A Case Study on Wilderness Management in a Changing World." The case for reintroduction was complicated and a challenge for environmental ethics. They explained how it is important to "acknowledge and understand all the values at stake" before coming to a conclusion.

They wrote about how our human understanding of wilderness has evolved over the years and that Isle Royale represents a "new, emerging development in that understanding." Wilderness policy is not a "simple, unquestionable, and inflexible dictate for nonintervention." The three authors also pointed out that humans have impacted nearly every landscape on the planet already.

Perhaps reintroduction was a viable option for saving the island ecosystem. After all, two prominent environmentalists, Aldo Leopold and Sigurd F. Olson, had supported introducing wolves in the 1940s. In fact, four captive-raised wolves were released in the park, unsuccessfully, in 1952. Three of them were killed or removed by humans. But this reintroduction would be different, and hopefully successful, because the wolves would be wild wolves, not captive-raised. It would be more like the impactful case of the 1995 Yellowstone wolf reintroduction.

When they wrote this paper in 2012, the island wolf population comprised just one pack, consisting of two females and a single male. The pack faced extinction, a condition Tim Cochrane referred to as "winking out." The decision of choosing to reintroduce wolves or not was growing more urgent.

The authors suggested three ways to proceed. The first, *wolf reintroduction*, involved bringing wolves

YELLOWSTONE'S SUCCESSFUL WOLF REINTRODUCTION

After decades of being hunted by humans, the last wolf pack in Yellowstone was killed in 1926. Without the wolves, the park and its wildlife suffered from overgrazing from the resident deer population. In 1995 and 1996, thirty-one gray wolves from Canada were brought to live in Yellowstone National Park. Another ten were added in 1997. After the wolves were reintroduced, the overgrazing stopped. Trees grew and forests developed. Songbird populations rose. Beaver returned and built dams, creating more pools in the rivers and greater numbers of wildlife. The reintroduction created a trophic cascade (a term that describes the changes in an ecosystem caused by the addition or removal of top predators), with all creatures benefiting.

This wolf, one of the animals reintroduced at Yellowstone, was photographed by a national park photographer from his vehicle. The wolves have enjoyed a successful return to the park.

to the island only if the population became extinct. In that case, researchers would introduce wolves to the island to establish a new population.

The second, *genetic rescue*, would introduce outside wolves to the island's existing small numbers in order to increase the genetic diversity of the existing population. This would address the concern that any wolf community on the island would require the diversity of genetic material from mainland wolves to succeed. This would strengthen the population and prevent extinction.

The third, *female reintroduction*, would consider bringing in female wolves to the island if only the male wolf was left alone on the island.

Each of these cases came with pros and cons. Debate persisted. In addition, others continued to voice objections to any wolf introduction. The three Isle Royale researchers refuted each argument. For example, in order to reintroduce caribou, thousands of moose would need to be removed. There were no plans to do that. Wolves are critical as long as moose are present on the island. They also countered the belief that wolves are "exotic" with the fact that wild-born wolves had occupied the island for years before any captive-bred wolves were ever brought to the island.

They concluded their discussion with the words of noted naturalist Aldo Leopold: "A thing is right when it tends to preserve the integrity, stability, and beauty of the biotic community. It is wrong when it tends otherwise." The plan to bring wolves

THE CASE FOR WOLVES

Wolves are a keystone species, meaning their presence is crucial to the entire ecosystem they're part of. Wolf expert Rolf Peterson mentioned the "green world hypothesis," which was first proposed in 1960 by three University of Michigan scientists, Nelson Hairston, Frederick Smith, and Lawrence Slobodkin. They suggested that meat-eating carnivores, like wolves, keep the world green because they limit the number of plant-eating herbivores, like moose.

"Carnivores, generally, are significant, even though they're rare," says Rolf. "It was a clever, short, three-page paper that was then debated for the next decade. I believe it. It's more true than not."

The green world hypothesis states that "herbivores are able to deplete the vegetation whenever they become numerous enough."

Wolves not only keep the plant-eating moose

under control on the island, but they also prey on other herbivores, including snowshoe hare and beaver. Fox, another island carnivore, also do their part in contributing to herbivore control. Wolves, however, are the top, or **apex**, **predators** on the island, with no natural predators of their own there.

it had to put its decision into action. Wolves would be captured on the mainland and brought to the island, beginning with relocating six to ten wolves as early as 2018.

The next step was to find wolves.

to the island would preserve the island's "integrity, stability, and beauty." Since wolves still inhabited the island, genetic rescue appeared to be the best solution.

This plan would give researchers a tool they could learn from and, depending on the success, use to possibly transform other threatened areas of the country in the future. In addition, the project would preserve the national park and the important predator-prey study for future generations.

After a lengthy environmental analysis, consultation with scientists, and input from the public, the National Park Service made its decision. Next,

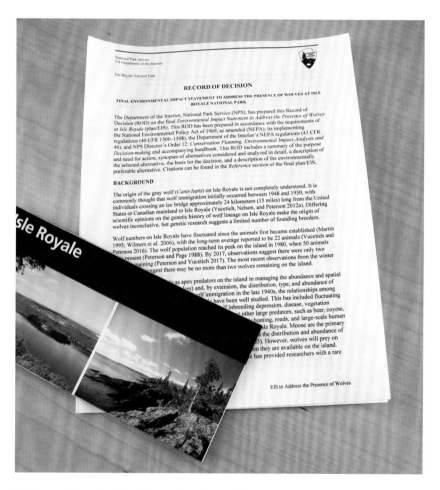

The formal Record of Decision to introduce wolves to Isle Royale National Park is signed.

WOLF CATCH AND RELEASE IS OFF AND RUNNING

THE SEARCH BEGAN FOR SUITABLE wild wolves in the Great Lakes region, including Minnesota tribal lands, and Ontario, Canada. The goal was to bring individual wolves from different pack territories for maximum genetic variety, according to chief of natural resources Mark Romanski. They searched to find healthy individuals between one and five years of age with clear eyes and strong canine teeth as indicators of good health.

The Isle Royale wolf recovery team of researchers and hired wranglers set out to capture and collar the wild wolves. They were fortunate to find a healthy pair on the first day on the Grand Portage Indian Reservation in Minnesota—a five-year-old male and a four-year-old female.

A veterinarian examines the teeth of one of the first captured wolves.

GRAY WOLF

Canis lupus
Mammal, canid, carnivore

WEIGHT: 70–110 pounds (32–50 kg)
HEIGHT: 2.5 feet (76 cm) on average
LENGTH: 3–5 feet (1–1.5 m), with a tail 1–2 feet (30–61 cm) long
AVERAGE LIFESPAN IN THE WILD: 5–9 years
STATUS: Endangered June 2019, delisted October 2020
FUN FACT: Wolves typically mate for life.

WOLF DIVERSITY

There are gray wolves (*Canis lupus*) and eastern wolves (*Canis* cf. *lycaon*) in the region. Ontario gray wolves are known to be quite large and experienced hunters. Minnesota wolves are not as big and have more eastern wolf DNA. Having a mixture of these different wolves will make the pack stronger, because their varied DNA will enable them to survive in difficult conditions.

An example of how increased genetic diversity provides strength can be seen right in your own garden. If you plant one species of potato and it develops a disease, you will lose your entire crop. That's what happened in Ireland during the Great Famine. But if you plant many varieties of potatoes, like farmers do in Peru, it is more likely that if one potato species falls to disease, other varieties will survive. Increasing the DNA diversity in the wolf population will help the wolves survive too.

EASTERN WOLF

(ALSO CALLED ALGONQUIN WOLF, AS OF 2016)

Canis lycaon
Mammal, canid, carnivore

WEIGHT: 55–65 pounds (25–29 kg)
HEIGHT: 2–2.6 feet (66–81 cm)
LENGTH: 3–5.2 feet (91–160 cm)
AVERAGE LIFESPAN IN THE WILD: 6–8 years
STATUS: Threatened
FUN FACT: An eastern wolf can reach a top speed of 39 mph (63 kmph).

THE BIG DAY

THE TEAM DIDN'T JUST FIND wolves, crate them, and set them free on Isle Royale. A wolf release isn't that easy. Ask United States Forest Service ecologist Lynette Potvin, who participated. On the initial date of the planned release in September 2018, Lynette's day started on Mott Island at seven a.m. Her head was full of questions. First, would the weather enable the release team to get to the opposite end of the largest island in the park, Isle Royale, where the release was planned?

The exact release site was yet to be decided, but she knew the general area. Lynette decided to hike to the drop-off point. But she couldn't hike there from Mott—it would take days. First she would need to sail to Siskiwit Bay, where her hike could begin.

The water was rough sailing from Mott Island to the bay, too rough to make it across the entire island to Windigo. She packed a sleeping bag and provisions, like food and extra clothes, because she

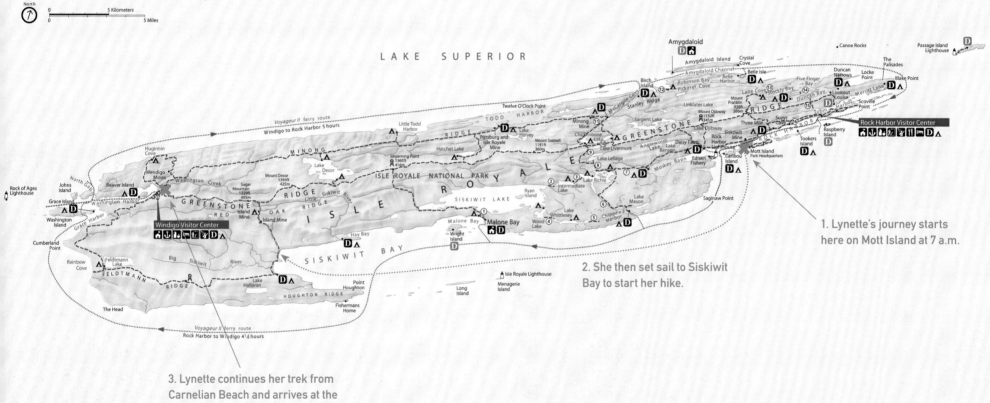

North

0 ___ 5 Kilometers
0 ___ 5 Miles

LAKE SUPERIOR

Amygdaloid
Amygdaloid Island
Amygdaloid Channel
Canoe Rocks
Passage Island Lighthouse
The Palisades
Crystal Cove
Belle Isle
Blake Point
Locke Point
Duncan Narrows
Birch Island
Robinson Bay
Pickerel Cove
Five Finger Bay
Lane Cove
Stockly Bay
Duncan Bay
Lookout Louise
Scoville Point
Twelve O'Clock Point
McCargoe Cove
Stanley Ridge
Linklater Lake
Mount Franklin
Mount Ojibway
Rock Harbor Visitor Center
Little Todd Harbor
Minong Mine
Sargent Lake
GREENSTONE
Lake Livermore
Lake Ojibway
Three Mile
Suzys Cave
Tobin
Merritt Lane
ROCK HARBOR
Raspberry Island
TODD HARBOR
RIDGE
Chickenbone Lake
Angleworm Lake
Daisy Farm
Rock Harbor Lighthouse
Siskiwit Mine
Hatchet Lake
Mount Siskiwit
Lake Harvey
RIDGE
Lake LeSage
Lake Benson
Moskey Basin
Edisen Fishery
Tookers Island
Ishpeming Point
Pittsburg and Isle Royale Mine
Lake Desor
Mount Desor
ISLE ROYALE NATIONAL PARK
Intermediate Lake
Lake Richie
Mott Island Park Headquarters
Caribou Island
Saginaw Point
MINONG
Sugar Mountain
Ryan Island
SISKIWIT LAKE
Lake Mason
Wendigo Mines
Red Oak Island Mine
Lake Whittlesey
Chippewa Harbor
Huginnin Cove
Washington Creek
Little Siskiwit River
Wood Lake
Beaver Island
GREENSTONE
RIDGE
Malone Bay
Washington Island
North Gap
Johns Island
Rock of Ages Lighthouse
Grace Island
Grace Harbor
Windigo Visitor Center
Wright Island
Hay Bay
Isle Royale Lighthouse
Menagerie Island
Cumberland Point
Washington Harbor
Voyageur II ferry route
Windigo to Rock Harbor 5 hours
SISKIWIT BAY
Point Houghton
Long Island
Rainbow Cove
Feldtmann Lake
FELDTMANN RIDGE
Big Siskiwit River
Lake Halloran
HOUGHTON RIDGE
Fishermans Home
The Head
Voyageur II ferry route
Rock Harbor to Windigo 4½ hours

1. Lynette's journey starts here on Mott Island at 7 a.m.

2. She then set sail to Siskiwit Bay to start her hike.

3. Lynette continues her trek from Carnelian Beach and arrives at the wolf drop-off point around 1 pm.

42

knew that she could get trapped on the island for days depending on the unpredictable fall weather. Lynette began her nine-mile hike inland from Carnelian Beach, on the far western side of Siskiwit Bay.

The wolf reintroduction team arrived with the first two wolves by air. Moose meat, harvested on the island the previous month, was placed out for the wolves. Not having to search for food would encourage the wolves to stay in certain areas of the island and help prevent any diseases or parasites from the mainland from entering the Isle Royale ecosystem.

The goal was to have a peaceful, quiet transition. After the reintroduction team opened the crates, placed in separate release sites away from the pair of native island wolves, the wolves sat for a bit, each listening, looking, and smelling their new habitat before leaping into freedom. The female left her crate first; the male waited until dark. Both went on to explore their new home and, hopefully, flourish.

Phyllis Green and Lynette Potvin open the crate for the historic release.

With ear tag and collar in place, the first female wolf takes her initial step onto Isle Royale.

But these new residents were different from the island's father/daughter duo. Unlike the original pair still left on the island, these new wolves had lived among packs that encountered human hunters on the mainland. They were skittish and wary of people. Those traits made them safer in their previous environment, but they were now living on an island without any hunters. While these wolves would adjust to this island, these traits, however, would now be passed on to any new packs that would form, possibly forever changing the unique relationship humans and wolves have shared on this island. While future island visitors might hear their howls at night, they may not get a glimpse of them during their stay.

This process of finding wolves and bringing

Researchers also use trail cameras to get insight into the behavior of the released wolves on the island. This photo of the first female wolf released was taken on September 27, 2018. You can see the collar around her neck that provides additional GPS information to the team.

them to the island was repeated over the course of the following months. Not all survived the stress of the capture-and-release process. "Although we do everything we can to quickly handle the animal and get them out to the island, of course, each animal is different," said Mark Romanski.

In response, the Park Service changed procedures to allow the wolves less time in captivity before their release. They decreased the time from up to forty-eight hours to less than twenty-four hours, in the hopes of alleviating the wolves' stress in captivity.

One female wolf, brought from Minnesota, decided the island wasn't for her, and on a rare day when an ice bridge did form, she took the opportunity to walk across the ice to Canada. If she had waited a day, she probably wouldn't have been able to do that, as the ice bridge disappeared. She was collared, so the team is still receiving location data from her since our visit. She's been on quite an adventure. After arriving in Canada, she ventured back into the United States and has been trekking miles. Although her movement does not influence the ongoing study of Isle Royale, her travels might lead to other insights into wolf behavior for the researchers.

By the end of March 2019, the population of wolves rose from two to fifteen. The new wolf residents were radio-collared and would be able to provide essential data to the team for roughly one to two years, or until the **GPS** batteries failed.

The female wolf's collar gives researchers a view into her early movements on the island. It shows that she visited the site where food was left within two hours of her release. She stayed there through the following morning, then moved northeastward.

WHEN DOES A GROUP OF WOLVES BECOME A PACK?

HOW WILL RESEARCHERS determine the success of this program? Scientific monitoring on Isle Royale is designed around assessing the result of this genetic rescue. Will these introduced wolves settle into the island and begin breeding? Not all of them, but there are hopes that most will. Once wolves form a group that travels together, hunts together, and sleeps close to each other, they are on the way to becoming a pack. It is not until they breed and have young together that the group is scientifically considered a pack. Pack formations will help determine the strategy's success.

We arrive on the island about six months after the last of the wolves were brought to the island from the mainland. The rehomed wolves had initially wandered around the island themselves, meeting up with each other and beginning to form

Not all wolves captured on the mainland are released on Isle Royale. This female, captured and collared in the Grand Portage area of Minnesota, didn't meet all the criteria for island release, but she will help to expand our knowledge of wolves going forward.

relationships. It's as if they were all kids brought into the same classroom. The kids start out possibly knowing one or two others, but after six months, they are a united group. Some may never get along, and others will form friendships that last for years or a lifetime. That's how it is with the wolves on Isle Royale. The researchers are like the classroom teacher, who gets to watch the group develop but doesn't always know the little individual things that go on with each relationship. The wolf collars help give more information to the researchers so that they can get a bigger picture of what is happening in terms of where the wolves are traveling, if they are traveling together, and where they are hunting, for example.

Ecologist Mark can't help but wonder about this class of wolves: "Probably the biggest curiosity in all of this is how they will actually form up and make packs. Some of the wolves arrive already knowing each other, but some come from different packs. At this point everybody is aware of each other. So that's one of the more interesting dynamics in all of this."

KEEPING TABS ON EVERYONE

PERHAPS THE GREATEST CHALLENGE FOR Mark Romanski, Isle Royale's chief of natural resources, is keeping tabs not only on the island's ecosystem but also on the volunteers, scientists, and National Park Service staff who have arrived for the summer months to conduct research.

Chief of natural resources for Isle Royale National Park Mark Romanski monitors the whereabouts of the newly released wolves and manages the island's researchers from his Mott Island office.

Mark lives and works on Mott Island from early May until the fall, then heads back to his mainland office in Houghton, Michigan, for the winter. On our visit, we find his Mott Island National Park office filled with data collection equipment used to oversee the twenty or so researchers in the field during the summer months, as well as the collared wolves and moose being studied. There are also coffee mugs and posters, collars and wildlife tags, and schedules and photos pinned to the walls.

Mark watches the comings and goings of the wolves from his standing desk with two computer monitors. Multiple maps fill the screens. And on each map are lots of dots—some are isolated and some are in clusters, indicating points where the wolves stopped and spent time. Each mark appears at a location on the map every time the GPS pings from the wolves' radio collars. The clusters are identified by wolf and map coordinates.

Mark shares the mapped coordinates with wildlife technicians, like Cara Ratterman. She'll use the GPS data from the collared animals to make field observations as part of a program in cooperation with the State University of New York College of Environmental Science and Forestry's Camp Fire Program in Wildlife Conservation. We'll get to see her use this data in action tomorrow.

Mark examines the maps of wolf coordinates that will later be used by wildlife technicians, like Cara, who will explore them in the field.

BE A WILDLIFE TECH

Job applicants hoping to work as seasonal Isle Royale wildlife techs like Cara Ratterman must be pursuing or have completed a degree in biology, wildlife science, ecology, or a similar field. They need to be able to follow strict data collection directions. Data collected should be accurate and filled out consistently on both field data sheets and digital forms.

But that's not all the job requires. Wildlife techs must be able to hike ten to fifteen miles (15 to 24 km) a day in remote backcountry using a GPS and while carrying a fifty-to-sixty-pound (23-to-27-kg) pack. Much of their work is done solo, so they must be able to live and work in the field by themselves.

The job description form also makes a point of mentioning that along with being self-motivated, flexible, and having a positive attitude, applicants also must possess a sense of humor. Do you have what it takes?

Cara has what it takes to be a wildlife tech, including a positive attitude in challenging conditions and enthusiasm for field discoveries—including scat collection.

Common loons, like this pair, sing us to sleep each evening.

USING TECHNOLOGY TO LEARN FROM SCAT AND FUR

MORGAN AND I ARE UP early to meet Mark Romanski's park research boat in Rock Harbor the next morning. A few of the loons we hear calling in the evenings swim about the docks while we wait. Their striking black and white plumage matches the opulence of their jewel-like red eyes.

It would be hard to pull us away from such a serene morning, but we're excited when Mark and wildlife tech Cara Ratterman arrive. They're taking us to a spot in Duncan Bay, where we'll go ashore to follow Cara as she investigates two clusters of pings from the radio-collared wolves that Mark has mapped. Together we'll search out a place where a potential alpha male Isle Royale wolf, #9, has spent some time and try to determine what he's been up to. An alpha male wolf will lead a pack. He's the first one to eat at a kill and dominates over the others. He will bond with a female and breed, producing pups for the pack.

Cara's been in the field since the beginning of May. Island field technicians go out with full packs of recording supplies, like plastic bags, gloves, trail cameras, GPS, and a radio. They also pack along food and often their camping gear. Boats transport them to some sites. Others are reached by hiking. Cara usually spends about five days in the field researching before returning with her samples.

Mark navigates the boat as close to the shore as possible to allow Cara, Morgan, and I to jump off and start our trek.

"We've seen a few moose predations in the last month, and we just started seeing Castor [beaver] predations. We've also seen some stranger predations, like fox den predations," Cara says about an earlier observation.

The fox predation points to a wolf or wolves that caught and killed a fox or fox kits at a den site. Wolves and fox are natural competitors. They hunt the same prey. It is not as common to record a predation that involved a wolf that has hunted a fox den.

When she finds a predation site, Cara records the location and places a motion-detection camera near the **carcass** so that researchers can monitor the decomposition, along with any visitors to the site. The cameras have documented ravens, fox, and eagles taking advantage of the scavenge opportunity. It's like the wolves have laid out a buffet for all the other island critters. They all benefit.

Once Cara returns with the GPS location of a moose carcass, the info is passed along to Rolf Peterson so that volunteers can later collect the remains to add to his ongoing study. Rolf's volunteers, through the moose-bone-collecting organization Moosewatch, will return to the site a year later, when all island creatures have had their fill and the bones are much cleaner, to acquire them for study.

Today, Cara will be out for just the day with us examining two clusters. Each has more than two dots, or pings, that create the cluster. Each ping indicates a spot the wolf has visited and stayed long enough for GPS to ping the location. A lot of pings in one area show that the wolf spent a considerable amount of time there. Was it perhaps catching and eating prey? Cara's job is part hiker, part detective, and part biologist.

Moose aren't the only species on the island with young in June. Canada geese won't abandon their goslings, even if their lives are under threat. These have found a safe spot in Rock Harbor.

After checking her gear. Cara hikes into the brush to the first ping location.

On the way to the bay, we spot lots of wildlife from the boat, including a variety of birds—geese, two bald eagles, loons, mergansers—and snowshoe hare. The boat is equipped with computer screens so that Mark can navigate the waters and let us off in a location near the first set of pings. He brings the boat perpendicular to an embankment and stops. Morgan, Cara, and I jump off the bow of the boat onto the dirt and scramble up the steep bank. We watch Mark motor away—the sound soon vanishes, leaving us again in the quiet of the islands.

There aren't any trails in this wilderness. It's time for us to bushwhack through to the first site, where there are three pings. We make our way through a maze of balsam branches and over fallen logs. It's thick with twigs and sticks and difficult, at times, to find a clear path.

Many of the fallen trees are the work of beaver, another island species that is changing the ecosystem by removing trees from the landscape to use in their dams and lodges.

AMERICAN BEAVER

Castor canadensis
Mammal, rodent, herbivore

WEIGHT: 40–70 pounds (18–32 kg)
LENGTH: 36–48 inches (91–122 cm), including tail,
 which is 10–16 inches (25–41 cm) long
AVERAGE LIFESPAN IN THE WILD: 10 years
STATUS: Common, but population threats exist in some areas
FUN FACT: Beaver can stay underwater for fifteen minutes.

Signs of busy beavers are all over.

Once we arrive at the top of the ridge where the pings indicate a wolf visit, Cara takes out a form to fill out. Our job is to search fifty meters in all directions, in pizza-slice formation. We're on the lookout for any signs, like scat (a scientific word for poop) and hairs, left behind. We start with the north and proceed through the pie slices.

Morning light glistens on spiderwebs and illuminates the green aspen and white birch in the canopy above. Loons call from the water below the ridge, breaking the quiet.

We locate samples of moose scat. There is also snowshoe hair scat, moose prints, and an area of the scratching marks on a tree branch where moose browsed. Morgan finds a space, at the base of a root, where digging took place. Cara puts on blue gloves, gets on her knees, and begins to sift through the dirt from the hole. There it is—a single wolf hair. She places it in a small manila envelope for lab testing. The hair will be analyzed to find out if it is the hair of the tagged alpha male wolf, #9, at this cluster site. It's not a great sample, but it's something.

COMMON LOON

Gavia immer
Bird, waterfowl, piscivore (feeds on fish)

WEIGHT: 9–12 pounds (4–5.4 kg)
LENGTH: 28–32 inches (71–81 cm)
AVERAGE LIFESPAN IN THE WILD: 10–25 years
STATUS: Threatened in Michigan
FUN FACT: Loons have four different calls.

If it is the tagged alpha wolf, then it confirms the ping of the collar that we are following. If it isn't, then it proves that another wolf, perhaps a wild-born uncollared wolf, visited the site as well. That could indicate a pair and the potential for a developing pack. More than likely, though, it will confirm the ping of the collared alpha male wolf, #9. The technology helps to solve some questions, but not all.

A few strands of hairs from a snowshoe hare are also found. All in all, there are four holes and a total of five strands collected for lab testing. There are no other signs of a struggle or bones left from any prey, so either the wolf took the prey somewhere else to feed on it, or the snowshoe hare got away. Cara records the GPS location of the site and places DNA samples in a drying compound, or desiccant, to keep them safe from any moisture and prevent degradation for testing.

We're on to the next site, identified as cluster #30. The clusters are numbered as they are identified by the pings from the wolf collars. This cluster is a bit farther along the ridge. More bushwhacking through the pines. More twigs that we snap and logs to climb over. This site proves a little more interesting. We locate a mound of moose scat, and on top of it we find a sample of wolf scat. Cara takes out a toothpick and scrapes along the sides of the wolf scat for epithelial cells, the cells on the outer skin, that have come off the skin of the wolf as it defecated, another scientific word for pooped. She places that toothpick in a container and gathers a second piece of the wolf scat for additional testing.

Lab tests will be able to determine a good deal of information, including diet and possible parasites. But that's not all we find at this site. There are two depressions—one on the ground beside two trees and another right next to it. Cara can tell by the size and shape that one is a moose bedding spot. It has depressions where the moose's elbows met the soft earth as it slept. Wolf scat and hairs indicate that the other smaller depression is a wolf bedding site. There are no signs of a struggle between the two. Perhaps the moose visited the site days before the wolf. Maybe the wolf tracked the moose there. Both are possibilities.

Cara radios Mark to return to pick us up. But before we hike back down the ridge, we stop to eat our packed lunches and enjoy the solitude of the site. We think about the moose and the wolf who bedded down in this same quiet spot. We didn't see them, but we felt their presence and saw evidence of their visit. Where were they now?

We've hiked farther from where Mark let us off in the morning, so we look for a safe spot for the boat to pick us up along the shoreline. With no

Wolf hairs help identify this site as a wolf bedding spot. They are collected for study.

dock again, Mark brings the boat close to the land, and we jump aboard the bow. On the ride back, he shows us a nearby beaver dam, which explains so many of the fallen trees. The sky, bright this morning, now blusters with wind. Clouds chase the boat to shore as the weather turns windy and wet. But the weather doesn't stay poor for long, and after a fish dinner, we're back on the hiking trails close to the lodge.

ISLAND MOOSE STUDIES

WE HIKE MILES OVER CLIFFS and beside ponds, but we don't see a single moose. The week is warm, and climate change is making it even warmer. The warming island makes it even more difficult for moose, which overheat, eat less, and suffer from an increased population of harmful ticks. These factors

Early June nights enable after-dinner hikes until close to 11 p.m.

impact all the moose, including the ones already weakened, bringing yet another stress to the island's wildlife.

The moose settle somewhere in the shade or hang out in ponds as the weather warms to keep cool. The ponds also provide them with nutritious aquatic plants to munch that contain more protein than plants growing on the land.

The plants growing in water also contain a valuable source of sodium that moose need. Most mammals take in sodium all year, but moose ingest large amounts only at certain times, mostly in early summer, as a supplement to their regular diet of branches and twigs. Their bodies store sodium for use during the colder months when these sources are unavailable. The heat takes its toll. If they do not eat enough when food is plentiful, they will have a difficult winter.

To further the moose-wolf studies on the island, in February of 2019, a helicopter team, along with a wildlife veterinarian and a wildlife research biologist, attached GPS collars to ten female moose

A moose and her calf cool down and grab a bite in an island lake.

on the island. Rolf Peterson worked as a spotter to locate the moose.

"These are cowboys," he said of the hired team that wrangles the moose or wolves. "The mugger is the one who jumps out of the aircraft to hold down the wolf or moose." It's not an easy role. Sometimes the tranquilizers do not have their full effect, and the animals are difficult to control. While fitting them with collars, the team also collected blood samples and examined each moose.

The collars give researchers the ability to compare the island moose population with the mainland population, providing them a window into predation behavior. Biologist Mark Romanski claims, "It also represents an opportunity to evaluate the impacts of restoring predation to the island ecosystem."

The research data the collars provide will shed light on these moose for years to come, offering opportunities for direct behavioral observations, information on the health of individuals, and insight into the island habitat. This important study might not only lead to more genetic rescues in other ecosystems but also help researchers manage wild areas during a period of environmental upheaval caused by the political disagreements over environmental protections and management in the midst of a warming planet.

While the moose collars provide data on the living population, researchers also work on learning from the deceased population. We need to board a small motorboat to take us to the center of that research—Bangsund Cabin.

BANGSUND RESEARCH STATION—LEARNING FROM MOOSE BONES

REACHING RESEARCHERS ROLF AND CANDY Peterson on the east end of Isle Royale is another challenge for another day. It requires renting a boat, watching the fast-changing Lake Superior weather, and traveling close to an hour to reach their nearest dock. We tie up the boat at the remains of an old fishing camp, whose owners were the Petersons' neighbors for years. The camp, now a historic site with information for visitors, gives us a glimpse into the lives of people who eked out a livelihood on these unpredictable waters.

We take a trail for roughly twenty minutes through the woods and over the island's cliffs to Bangsund Cabin, where a welcoming sign greets park visitors at the end of the path. The cabin is the summer field headquarters for the Isle Royale wolf-moose research project, a launching point for Moosewatch volunteer groups, and the Petersons' home base during the season.

The Edisen Fishery, now a historic site, was home to Rolf and Candy Peterson's neighbors for years.

Bangsund Cabin is the summer field headquarters for the world's longest predator/prey study and the summer home for researchers Rolf and Candy Peterson.

Like an outdoor curiosity cabinet or natural history museum, a display of moose skulls and jawbones lining the lakeside shelves outside of Bangsund Cabin catches our eye. Some are bleached white from years of sunshine exposure, others covered in patches of green moss, and more recently had their skin and fur removed.

Candy and Rolf step out of the small log cabin, with its red window frames, to greet us.

Apron-clad Candy takes a break from meal prep for the volunteers, who will be arriving soon. She points to the display. "All the bones you see here are bones that were collected this year. This is two weeks' worth of effort."

She's referring to the bones collected by Moosewatch volunteers, who spend weeks in the field retrieving moose bones for the study. The third party of the season will return tomorrow, deliver their finds, and camp at the site with Candy and Rolf before they head home.

"I love the days when the group goes out in the woods, but I love when they come back. They come back as a group," says Candy.

The volunteers arrive at Isle Royale from all over the country, but they share a common desire to be in the wild and help the project. As Candy notes, they start their time there as individuals, not knowing each other. After a week in the field, in all weather, they form a tightly knit community.

The skulls she's pointed to on the shelves include the bones of moose that recently died and others who perished years earlier. "Some died twenty years ago," says Candy.

Candy preps a meal for the Moosewatch volunteers, who will be returning with more bones tomorrow.

Rolf can determine when a moose died by examining the bones.

The groups don't know what they'll find in the wild. The collection from this year also includes bones that have been in the wilderness for forty years and longer, but Candy notes that those aren't on display because they're too fragile.

Rolf picks up a skull. "But a good portion have died this winter, because the groups are going to points that the GPS have indicated in wolf cluster pings," he says. Those clusters, as we saw in Mark's office and explored with Cara, give researchers a view into predation sites and locations for moose bone retrieval.

But not all of these moose were preyed upon by wolves. Since the reintroductions just started in 2018, there were many years without enough wolves to prey on the moose. Many of them died from starvation. Rolf and Candy can tell by the weathering of the bones and the smell which ones have died more recently.

The moose volunteers come from all over the country to participate in this study. It's important that they love to backpack, because they go out for seven days at a time, covering miles on and off the trails to retrieve these bones. Rolf keeps in touch with all the Moosewatch teams while they are out in the field through texts from special satellite devices.

Two strings of moose vertebrae bones hang from a tree branch. In the back of the long benches, on the other side of a small shed, is the "antler graveyard." Moose grow antlers every year, shedding the old, but the bones in this collection feature abnormal skulls. There are record-breaking old moose skulls, skulls with strange antler growth, and other abnormalities. It's like a Ripley's Believe It or Not! of moose skulls and antlers.

The collected skulls from this year will be cleaned by Rolf and bleached in the sunshine before going to a mainland archival facility for storage.

Why collect all these bones? The bones tell stories—moose that have died from broken legs, disease, starvation. Studying and comparing the skulls and bones year after year provides even more information. Ecologists from Michigan Technological University compared skull measurements on 662 skulls from over forty years of Isle Royale bone collections. They can take those measurements and discover the health of a population and changes in the environment over those years. One question they are investigating: Is climate warming impacting moose?

They found that the skulls decreased in size over the forty years. They also found that when moose calves experienced a warm first winter, they became smaller adults and lived shorter lives. Now, through continued research, scientists can work on finding out why that is happening and what it may mean for future herds as the global temperature continues to rise.

Examination of front **incisors** on lower jaws helps estimate the age of the moose. Teeth can be cut in half to show rings, like tree rings, that are counted to determine a moose's age. Peterson has studied both moose and wolf teeth on the island. He's found evidence of fossil fuel burning and radioactive fallout that occurred during above-ground testing prior to the Nuclear Test Ban Treaty of 1963 in wolf teeth, demonstrating how human development impacts wildlife on a cellular level.

While we're outside listening to the Petersons discuss the wolf/moose study, two kayakers hike over to join us. The cabin is a welcoming spot for all park visitors. Candy invites us all into the cabin, where she has a tray of fresh-baked brownies for everyone to sample, a guest book to sign, and walls papered with photos and articles to read. Her

lasagna for tomorrow's volunteers is baking in the oven and fills the cabin with a delicious smell.

The group of us begin sharing experiences of our time on the island. The small cabin is warm and comfortable, but I can see how challenging it must have been for the Petersons raising two young boys in this isolated spot during the summers, without many modern conveniences, decades ago. Frequently, Rolf was out in the field, collecting data on Isle Royale, and Candy was there alone with her sons. But the isolation on the islands was also a gift. One

Sweet treats and a guestbook await all the visitors to the cabin, but the best part is hearing Candy speak about her experiences on the island.

Rolf and Candy Peterson's sons grew up spending summers at the lakeside cabin with their parents.

Michigan Tech, the National Park Service, the wolf-moose project, and other groups. Izzy and Tom Offer-Westort, a former Michigan Tech grad student, are two of the researchers on this moose-browsing observation project.

When we leave Rolf and Candy that afternoon, we steer our boat across the lake to check out Izzy Evavold's research firsthand.

of their children became so knowledgeable about the island and its wildlife that, as a teen, he even filled in as a guide for a weeklong expedition.

Outside, Rolf takes a look through his scope pointed across the lake at Daisy Farm, where researcher Izzy Evavold is spending time today observing live collared moose.

Like the other researchers on Isle Royale, Izzy collects data that stretches into many studies. Izzy's particular study is part of a joint project among

We leave Rolf and Candy at their cabin, knowing that tomorrow there will be more visitors, more volunteers, and more bones.

JOIN A MOOSEWATCH EXPEDITION

The research going on in Isle Royale National Park doesn't just involve traditional scientists. Citizen-scientist volunteers make significant contributions when they join a Moosewatch expedition.

Accepted applicants are greeted at the ferry dock at Rock Harbor and spend several hours in orientation with Rolf and Candy. Training happens, and then food and equipment are packed. Volunteers spend the next week in the backcountry of Isle Royale, searching for moose bones with the help of GPS coordinates. Hiking several miles each day, the team follows animal trails and camps each night in the wilderness, in all weather, including buggy conditions. Moose bones are located, collected, and carried back, along with reports of the find. Some have been picked clean by scavengers and are easy to transport. In contrast, others are more freshly deceased, with decomposing flesh still attached, and need to be wrapped in plastic for transport.

When volunteers set off, their packs start at

Behind Bangsund Cabin is the Boneyard, a collection of interesting moose-skull oddities collected over the years.

about forty pounds (18 kg) each, but by the time the group arrives back at Bangsund Cabin with moose bones, those packs can be fifty-five to sixty pounds (25 to 27 kg). After the group returns and unloads their gear and the bones they collected all week, they're treated to showers, a hot meal, and camping at the cabin.

Moosewatch groups begin heading out in early May, proceed until midsummer (when the bugs take over the island and make work conditions even more difficult), and then return in early fall, finishing up before the park closes for the year.

Ron Porritt participated in four Moosewatch sessions, starting in 2013. "Moosewatch gives an opportunity to be part of something that is meaningful beyond self. It really is important that we understand this nature/man/ecosystem thing we are part of," he says.

Ron's had many adventures during each of those sessions, including locating a "fresh kill" in 2018 of a moose recently deceased. "The moose was complete. . . . We stretched out her leg, placed the femur on top of a large rock, and used another large rock to break into the bone, exposing a marrow that was depleted of fat—indicating starvation." These finds enable participants to make important discoveries that benefit the long-term research of the island. Ron always leaves his time on Isle Royale feeling enriched and looking toward the future of our wild lands.

"What we [Americans] do with our wild lands is not at all well-defined, and it is our youth that will determine what endures beyond us. Isle Royale is almost entirely 'wilderness.' If you can help get youth interested in this one wilderness, you will do a service to all of our wild lands," says Ron.

In 2019, the first all-women expedition occurred, led by Loreen Niewenhuis. Over the 2019 season, groups of seventy-seven volunteers, with five researchers, hiked over one thousand miles on the islands to uncover the remains of over one hundred dead moose. The bones they collected will lead to continued research and understanding of the wolves and moose of Isle Royale.

Male moose grow antlers each spring and shed them each winter. Their antlers are used for defense and for attracting a mate.

LIVE MOOSE WATCHING

WE SPOT INTERN IZZY EVAVOLD'S bright pink jacket as our boat gets closer, and she's holding something that resembles an old television branched antenna. Izzy is using telemetry to track moose signals. Just like the wolf collars, the moose collars send out signals until batteries wear out or the collar is destroyed. By listening to the sounds the telemetry antenna generates when a moose is in the vicinity, Izzy can identify the moose in the field. The louder the sound, the closer the moose is to the person tracking. If the beeping sound remains still, Izzy knows the moose is staying put. When she locates a moose, she can attempt to find it and observe it. Unlike with GPS, Izzy must pick up the signal from three locations to narrow her search. Telemetry, which is more cost-effective than GPS, involves a radio transmitter, antenna, and a receiver. The first signal she receives tells her that a moose is in the vicinity, but not which direction. She then moves to another point to pick up the signal. The beeping sound gets closer as she narrows in on the animal's location. If she moves away from the animal, then the signal isn't heard. The moose isn't always standing still, waiting for Izzy to come and find it! Often the moose is moving about and can't be located by sight.

We miss a moose sighting that afternoon at Daisy Farm, but we do get the chance to speak with Izzy about her month of research. After we tie our boat up, she shares that this is her third year

Intern Izzy Evavold uses telemetry to pick up the signals of collared moose in the area to observe.

collecting field data for the wolf-moose project and her tenth visit to the park. She's been observing radio-collared moose since her May arrival to learn how moose make decisions about where to feed. Moose love munching on balsam but do not like spruce. Isle Royale has both. The arrival of the new wolves might prove risky for some of those habitats and result in a shift of current moose behavior. What happens if the wolves hang out where the moose like to eat? Where will the moose go? Izzy's there to investigate.

"This was the second time I had worked with the predator-prey study, once in the summer of 2018 measuring the impact of moose on balsam fir trees, and this month recording moose behavior," she says.

Izzy will finish her undergraduate degree in wild-life biology this spring at the University of Montana. But she'll still be involved with the study upon her return to school, because she's using the behavioral data and other data recorded by the moose collars as part of her senior thesis project. She's focusing on trying to determine if moose change behavior due to seasonality and temperature.

The moose collars provide a location, along with **accelerometer** data, which indicates the moose's movement. It measures up-down movements as well as right-to-left and backward-forward motion. This data enables Izzy and other researchers to identify if the moose if foraging for food or just resting. Izzy will take that data and then apply it to the temperature to be able to plot behavior during the change in seasons and between night and day.

Izzy had some memorable moments during her month on the island as a seasonal Balsam Fir Intern, whose sole purpose is observing munching moose. She shared one such encounter she had just days before she met us.

"The first was when I spotted moose #17, which I had nicknamed Abba, as a distant silhouette of moose ears hiding in the shade of a spruce tree," says Izzy. This was on one of her final days as a moose observer, so she was hoping to get a good observation to finish out her time on the island. By "a good observation," Izzy means that she was hoping for a clear visual for an extended time before the moose noticed her there.

Most of her observations occurred a few hundred feet (100 m) or more from the animal, but this time was different. Abba was much closer—probably only about two hundred feet (60 m) or so from where Izzy was crouched down, out of sight, on a slightly rocky rise behind some shrubs. She viewed the moose with binoculars.

"I was able to watch her for an hour or so as she rested, got up, and started eating. She slowly made her way in my direction but luckily never detected me." This enabled Izzy to complete observing the moose's behavior without interruption.

She continued, "I was close enough to hear her chew and strip buds and leaves off of branches. Eventually, she wandered off, still unaware I had watched her for so long."

Izzy took notes of all her observations. She also had an unforgettable observation of a younger moose—a yearling male called a bull who wasn't collared.

"Since I didn't have a way to identify the moose by collar number, I thought "Velvety Buttons" was accurate, since he had small, velvet-covered bumps

Izzy holds the radio receiver and antenna, while the moose is tagged with the transmitter.

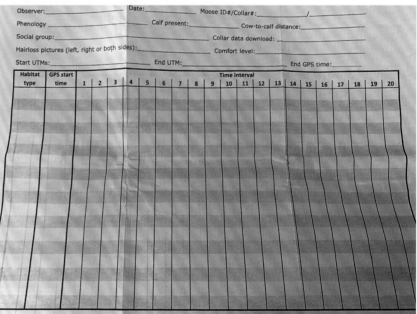

Data sheets are an important tool in recording field observations.

that were his first antlers. I'm pretty sure I ran into this moose three or four times in the month I was working; he almost always was between me and where moose #17 was. Once, I saw him resting and watched for a while. He was pretty relaxed, so I got to see him yawn and try not to nod off."

Izzy continues her recollection of seeing this little bull. "Another time he was resting and laid his head down on the ground briefly to sleep, I think. I was pretty far away from him, but I think he knew I was there and slept anyway. It's likely I saw different moose, but I'm fairly certain it was the same one based on his antler size."

Not unlike hikers who walk the trails of Isle Royale for many hours, researchers in the field observe much more than their intended subject. Izzy's time on wild Isle Royale was no

exception. She'll never forget a chance meeting she had with one of the island's other predators—a fox.

"I remember a fox that trotted right between me and my tent when [fellow researcher] Tom and I camped off-trail to get closer to where some collared moose were. We were maybe a mile from the

This snowshoe hare didn't care that we were hiking on this boardwalk. It hopped right along toward us. This is a benefit to having a wildlife community that isn't hunted and fearful of humans.

SNOWSHOE HARE

Lepus americanus
Mammal, lagomorph, herbivore

WEIGHT: 3–4 pounds (1.4–1.8 kg)
LENGTH: 18–20 inches (21–51 cm)
LIFESPAN: Can live as long as 5 years in the wild, but many die before that
STATUS: Common
FUN FACT: Their fur color changes with the seasons to provide camouflage.

nearest trail, and the fox didn't even hesitate walking right past us."

Those unusual encounters don't just happen to researchers. Morgan and I had one ourselves while we were hiking on the island when a snowshoe hare came hopping toward us along a thin plywood plank over a marshy area of a trail.

These unexpected moments make Isle Royale all the more special. Because the island is so isolated and hunting is prohibited, wildlife tends not to be as skittish as they might be on the more populated mainland. It always helps to be extra quiet when hiking and to pause to allow for those experiences to happen.

But even being on the island for countless hours each day didn't make observing wildlife easy for Izzy or us. The researcher didn't have many observations the week we met her on the island.

"Each observation had to be made without being detected by the moose [smelled, seen, or heard]. So we had to be pretty far away and be in the right place at the right time to get a good observation. That's why we had so few behavior categories, because we were too far away usually to detect or see more specific behaviors. Most days, neither Tom nor I would get an observation in because we would spook our moose or would run out of time in the day trying to locate and quietly approach the moose."

It's nearing the time we need to return the boat to the harbor and grab dinner before the island's only restaurant closes for the night. Izzy is packing up to leave too.

But the long days still afford us all with hours before the sun sets at around eleven p.m. A hike along the rocky shore is planned for after dinner, before the evening loon serenades and lapping waves lull us to sleep.

Isle Royale's rocky shoreline

MOOSE SCAT

Not more than ten steps onto our very first hiking trail, the day we arrived in Isle Royale, we experienced our first moose-poop-pellet sighting. We were ecstatic. We knew we were in moose territory. There was proof! Moose poop resembles deer scat: it's a pile of pellets, except moose scat is much larger. The piles soon became an ordinary occurrence. They were everywhere on the island and hard to avoid when hiking.

What do these piles tell scientists? They enable researchers to learn a lot, including basic health and dietary patterns. Moose need to eat about forty pounds (18 kg) of vegetation each day to maintain their health. But what are they eating? And do they make choices?

"You'd think if you had such dietary require-ments, you'd stuff your face with anything you can find, but that doesn't appear to be the case," says Sarah Hoy, research assistant professor at Michigan Tech, who works with the samples.

Think about how you eat. How would your body feel if you ate only your favorite food? Probably not good. After a while, your body would crave other foods so that you received the nutrition you need, or you'd get sick. And what would you eat if you knew you had to compete in a sport? You would probably eat accordingly, maybe more carbohydrates.

Moose are similar. They love balsam, but they don't eat just balsam. Researchers from Michigan Tech found that moose prefer to eat what is somewhat rare or limited in their habitat. For example, if balsam is rare, they'd prefer it and gobble it up. If it is common, they will pass it up to find a less common plant to include in their diet. Rare, limited foods add

You can tell there are plenty of moose around even if you don't see them. Their scat is everywhere.

nutritional diversity. Imagine that your school cafeteria has only PB&J for lunch every day. And then on Fridays they also have pizza. There might be a rush from students to buy pizza, because it isn't available all the time. That's what the moose do with their food sources. They prefer the items they can't find all the time.

Preferences aside, researchers find that moose are less fussy about what they eat when they risk being attacked by wolves or when deep snow makes it difficult to locate other food options.

Moose scat can also provide scientists with important information about the health of the moose population.

CANDY'S CIRCUS

LET'S RETURN TO CANDY'S CIRCUS analogy. Is the island a living laboratory or a circus? Candy believes it's a circus, and we all come to it for different reasons. Some come for the moose-wolf drama in one of "several rings." Others watch the clowns, like the playful otters that Candy and Rolf often see frolicking on the shore near Bangsund Cabin. Everyone has a role. The wolves, moose, beaver, snowshoe hare, and squirrels all go about their own lives in the different tents or rings, with us observing.

And many of the humans have jobs. Candy points to the rangers, who act like ushers, the park maintenance workers, who make sure the seats work, and the others who help visitors understand and appreciate everything. But we, along with all the other humans, are "the observers." Candy says, "That is our role, and it is an important role. What is the point of the play if the audience isn't there to see it?"

RED FOX

Vulpes vulpes
Mammal, canid, carnivore

WEIGHT: 5—31 pounds (2—14 kg)
HEIGHT: 14—20 inches (36—51 cm)
LENGTH: 18—35 inches (46—89 cm)
AVERAGE LIFESPAN IN THE WILD: 2—5 years
STATUS: Stable
FUN FACT: Red fox were first spotted on the island in 1925.

The sun is shining above Bangsund Cabin, and a bird calls over her words, as Candy explains. "Our role in creation is to honor the rest as no other animal can, and to stand back from all of it and say, 'Wow, isn't it neat?' and be grateful for it. And we need to take responsibility for the island and keep it going."

Rolf and Candy discuss whether the island can be described as a living laboratory or a circus.

Rolf lets Candy finish her thoughts. "Some say we don't have a role in nature, but hey, when did we get written out of the cast of characters?" she asks. "We are needed now more than ever to fix our mistakes. We've done some bloopers."

That's exactly what is being done by reintroducing wolves back to the natural environment of Isle Royale: attempting to fix some bloopers.

Candy moves on to some essential features of Isle Royale National Park. No one possesses the island circus. We do, however, own the national park. We all can enjoy our *oohs* and *aahs*. The performing animals on the island we share are protected by law. And she says that sometimes we are so overwhelmed by what we see in the circus that we "might even rush out for a moment into the ring." But the "trick is to know when to return to our seats."

What do you think? Is the island a "living laboratory" or is it a "circus"? Or is it both?

OTHER ISLAND WILDLIFE

ISLAND ISOLATION HAS CONTRIBUTED TO the number and diversity of animal species calling Isle Royale home. To get here, somehow the animals have had to find their way across the cold, deep waters to the island shores.

Some animals, like the wolves, initially crossed over the frozen lake from Canada. For others, the

Only two snake species are found on Isle Royale—
the northern red-bellied and this one, the common garter snake.

journey is less clear because of their longevity on the island. Snowshoe hare, beaver, muskrat, red squirrels, and deer mice have been present for thousands of years. The Isle Royale red squirrel, Isle Royale deer mouse, and the American marten have evolved into distinct species over that time.

Take the island's tiny red squirrels. They are everywhere. No one is sure how they arrived on the island, but we can see that the isolation has impacted the species. Because of the long period it has lived on the island without relatives, it is now considered a **subspecies** (*regalis*) of the red squirrel. It is smaller and less red than its relatives on the mainland.

Beaver are the largest rodents on Isle Royale. Prolific swimmers, they probably arrived by swimming to the island. When still called Minong, the island was known for having large beaver, larger than any left on the mainland. Ojibwa hunters trapped beaver by breaking up their lodges and taking them out by hand as they fled into the water. Tim Cochrane noted this in his book *Minong: The Good Place*, wherein he also observed that 849 beaver skins were traded at Fort William from the area in 1816.

The beaver population has climbed in the last few years from 250 to roughly 450. Each lodge they construct is home to between two and eight beaver.

EASTERN GREAT HORNED OWL

Bubo virginianus
Bird, carnivore

WEIGHT: 2—5.5 pounds (0.9—2.5 kg)
LENGTH: 18—25 inches (46—63 cm)
WINGSPAN: 3.3—4.8 feet (1—1.5 m)
AVERAGE LIFESPAN IN THE WILD: 13 years
STATUS: Common
FUN FACT: Feather tufts on their heads are often called "plumicorns."

With the increase in population, beaver are felling greater numbers of trees in areas where they decide to build homes. Beaver are able to transform open areas and forests into large ponds, dramatically altering the landscape and habitat. This was another strong reason for introducing wolves to maintain the island ecosystem and prey on beaver as well as moose.

Visitors can't miss seeing a snowshoe hare in the park. And yet the numbers have decreased since the wolves have been reintroduced. Their numbers peaked around 2014-15, when there were around ten times the amount as now. While their population soared with so few predators, one predator's numbers rose—great horned owls.

But now that the hare population has lowered, so has the owl population. This is another example of how predator and prey numbers impact each other in an ecosystem.

"There is a sensitive balance," says Rolf, between these species populations. When one thing changes, the balance shifts. But the ecosystem is also resilient. **Carnivores** keep the herbivores in check.

LOOKING INTO THE CRYSTAL BALL

FOR NOW, IT'S OUR TIME to leave this living laboratory, or wild circus, depending on your view. While Morgan and I wait on the dock to board the *Ranger III* for our voyage back to Houghton, an excited couple tells us about a moose they just saw munching beside the trail nearby. The two of us take off running to see if we can catch a glimpse before we leave. Alas, it has moved on, and we are left to wander back to the dock and walk up the gangplank into the ship. We drop our bags and head to the outside deck to get our last views of the island as we sail away.

We leave behind the researchers who continue to observe and record the goings-on of Isle Royale wildlife. We know that the ecosystem of the island is not yet fully restored to a healthy number of moose, but we have hope that the wolves brought to the island will set it all in balance again.

A bull moose on the Rock Harbor trail is spotted but, unfortunately, not by us.

Months later, we hear good news. By the end of 2019, the wolves that were relocated to Isle Royale were eating well. There were fifteen wolves on the island at the end of that year, eight males and seven females. The study documented 381 kills, with wolves feeding on moose, beaver, and snowshoe hare.

More good news! At the beginning of 2020, a potential pack was reported. Two males and one female were traveling together and defending their territory. It was later reported that pups were born on the island. The exact number wasn't known, but it looks as if a pack has formed, meaning that the introduction of wolves to the island can be deemed a success!

But that doesn't stop the program. The goal is to introduce more wolves to the island. Mark isn't sure when or where other wolves will be relocated. "In terms of future relocation events, it will be dependent on what is happening that day and whether or not we are able to access areas of the park based on weather and personnel and what the wolves are doing. It's all a balance."

Lynette adds the other factors that impact relocation: "Weather also dictates where we can release the wolves. We're also restricted by where the planes can land."

In the meantime, a limited number of researchers study the island during the winter months when the island is closed to the general public and the ships are not in service. The winter of 2019 also led to the discovery of the death of the last original male wolf left on the island, whose ancestors were affectionally called Old Gray Guy and Cinderella.

"The Old Gray Guy, who came across an ice bridge and introduced new genes into the population, and Cinderella, a notable alpha who survived a pack coup, are important examples. And the recovery of this carcass from the last known male wolf of the previous populations may well prove to be another important example," said John Vucetich, professor of ecology and a Winter Study leader. These are examples of how important genetic diversity is to the island ecosystem. Those genes that were introduced into the ecosystem might have just saved the last two wolves, which weren't infected by the canine parvo disease that killed the others.

The twelve-year-old male wolf, known as W004F, died in 2019 of wolf-inflicted wounds. At the time of our visit, his daughter was believed to be still alive on the island. Wolves live on average six to eight years in the wild but have been known to live up to thirteen years. Wolf-on-wolf aggression is common as wolves defend and establish territories and social hierarchy. Researchers can now study the remains of wolf W004F and his DNA.

THE LESSON OF ISLE ROYALE

EVERY INCH OF OUR PLANET has been impacted in some way by humans, even our most remote wilderness. What is our relationship going to be with these wild areas in the future? Can we intervene in time to protect them?

The remote Isle Royale National Park provides a place that is one of our wildest national parks. It is one of the few or only spots on the planet that is inhabited by a top predator that isn't hunted and persecuted, a large herbivore that is also not hunted, and a forest that is protected from logging. That certainly makes it a special place, deserving consideration and conservation.

Isle Royale can serve as a laboratory for scientists to learn how to manage many of the other wild areas. If the park's wolf reintroduction program is as successful as Yellowstone's, it can provide even more information for how we deal with earth's other wild areas in the future. Isle Royale can show us how to repair a damaged ecosystem. It might even show us how to revive an endangered species.

Our world is going through a climate crisis. Lake Superior is one of the world's fastest warming lakes. Its summer surface temperatures have increased twice as much as air temperatures since 1980, and the sun-warmed upper layer of the water extends farther into the depth of water. We will need the knowledge and data that these studies provide us—both the ones that failed and the ones that were successful—for maintaining our biodiversity and keeping our wild areas living, breathing, healthy ecosystems.

As Morgan and I leave Isle Royale, I remember that this is one of the least visited national parks, yet so many return to it again and again. Having explored its serene trails and glimpsed its elusive, fascinating wildlife, I hope to return, too. Of course, Longstreth's writing also pops into my head. He wrote in 1924, "I HESITATE to write about Isle Royale with the enthusiasm that I feel, for enthusiasm, they say, is contagious, and contagion is the very thing I should like to spare the place. Were I to write as I would of the Isle, every reader would drop the book and ring for his boat."

We do have to keep in mind that sometimes we over-love our wild places. To that end, we need to preserve and protect them, even while learning from them. I hope this **rewilding** experiment is permitted to continue with minimal human interference and succeeds in restoring the balance of this special and unique island of tilted rocks.

Nobody knows what the future of Isle Royale National Park holds, but we have met the dedicated scientists, researchers, and staff who are focused on its survival. And it's in good hands.

GLOSSARY

accelerometer—An instrument that measures movement. Collars that are attached to an animal include this instrument to detect and record the animal's full range of motion.

apex predator—The top predator in a food chain. Wolves are the apex predators on Isle Royale.

archipelago—A group of islands that form a cluster or chain. Isle Royale National Park is a cluster of over 450 islands.

boreal forest—A forest growing in the Northern Hemisphere that is made up of mostly cold-tolerant coniferous (cone-bearing) tree species, such as balsam fir and white spruce. Paper birch and aspen also grow along the rugged island boreal forests. Lake Superior's cool waters create the cool, moist conditions that favor growth of boreal forests.

carcass—The dead body of an animal. Carcasses that are left behind after a wolf kill are picked over by scavengers, including ravens and fox.

carnivore—A meat-eating animal. Wolves and fox are two carnivore species living on Isle Royale.

carrying capacity—The number of individuals that a place can support without environmental degradation.

ecosystem—A biological community of living things in their physical environment that are interdependent.

extirpated—Wiped out from an area, like a localized extinction. Many animal species can be extirpated from an area by hunters or other forces.

GPS—Global positioning system. This navigational system uses satellites to fix the location of a radio receiver on or above the earth. We use GPS systems in our cell phones and televisions. Researchers on Isle Royale use GPS to communicate with each other and to track wolves and moose.

herbivore—An animal that eats plants. Moose and snowshoe hare are examples of Isle Royale herbivores.

incisor—A tooth found in the front of the mouth, sometimes called an eyetooth.

keystone species—A species that is vital to an entire ecosystem. The ecosystem would be threatened if that species is removed.

polar vortex—A mass of cold air that sits over the North (or South) Pole and, when displaced, can bring arctic temperatures southward. The polar vortex can deliver subzero temperatures to the United States and Canada for a week or more at a time. Some scientists believe that the melting sea ice in the arctic might be responsible for more frequent changes in the polar vortex.

predator—An animal that preys on other animals to obtain food. Wolves are the major predator on Isle Royale, but fox are also an island predator. Eagles and owls are Isle Royale predators too.

prey—Animals that are killed for food by a predator. Snowshoe hare and moose, both herbivores, are prey for wolves on Isle Royale.

rewilding—Reintroducing a species into a former territory. The rewilding of wolves to Isle Royale reintroduced a species that was in danger of being extirpated from the islands.

subspecies—A subdivision member branch of a species.

telemetry—The transmission of radio signals between a radio collar and a receiver device. Researchers on Isle Royale use telemetry to track radio-collared moose.

FOR MORE INFORMATION

READ:

Castaldo, Nancy F. *Back from the Brink: Saving Animals From Extinction*. Boston, MA: Houghton Mifflin Harcourt, 2018.

Peterson, Rolf Olin. *The Wolves of Isle Royale: A Broken Balance*. Ann Arbor: University of Michigan Press, 2007.

Raycroft, Mark. *Moose: Crowned Giant of the Northern Wilderness*. Richmond Hill, ON, Canada: Firefly Books, 2017.

Swinburne, Stephen R., and Jim Brandenburg. *Once a Wolf: How Wildlife Biologists Fought to Bring Back the Gray Wolf*. Boston, MA: Houghton Mifflin Harcourt, 2001.

WATCH:

"The Wolves and Moose of Isle Royale"—Take a look into the study produced by Michigan Tech. www.youtube.com/watch?v=PdwnfPurXcs

"The Wolves of Yellowstone"—Learn more about the wolf reintroduction project at Yellowstone. ny.pbslearningmedia.org/resource/a58e3ca2-52ab-45f5-87ac-26ee0d681146/wolves-of-yellowstone-earth-a-new-wild

EXPLORE:

Isle Royale National Park Page: www.nps.gov/isro/index.htm

See the statistics of moose and wolf numbers: www.nps.gov/isro/learn/nature/wolf-moose-populations.htm

Moosewatch expedition: isleroyalewolf.org/participate/participate/explorers.html

Wolves & Moose of Isle Royale Study: isleroyalewolf.org

DO:
JOURNAL YOUR OBSERVATIONS LIKE AN ISLAND RESEARCHER

You can keep a nature journal of your observations, just like the researchers do on Isle Royale, no matter where you live. All you need is a notebook and a pencil to start with. Begin by recording the weather each day. Include more than just the temperature. Identify the clouds in the sky, the rainfall, and whether it is windy or not.

What birds do you see? Can you identify the species? Learn to use field guides to help you with species identification. As you learn more, you might even be able to identify and record bird songs.

Record any other animals you see during your day, including insects. Write down the behavior you spot, like Izzy's descriptions of her moose sightings.

Don't forget to include plant observations. Are the trees changing color or dropping leaves? Are flowers blooming? Add sketches, leaf rubbings, and watercolors of what you see.

Lastly, write down your feelings. Were you excited by an animal you've never seen before?

Whether you decide to keep a daily, weekly, or monthly nature journal, you'll have an opportunity to make discoveries and witness changes to our environment in real time.

SOURCE NOTES & BIBLIOGRAPHY

SOURCE NOTES

12 "This shard of a continent becalmed": Longstreth, *Lake Superior Country*, 313–14.

15 "where the animals you are counting and studying do not wander away": Allen, *Wolves of Minong*, xviii.

35 "acknowledge and understand all the values at stake": Vucetich, Nelson, and Peterson, "Should Isle Royale Wolves Be Reintroduced?" 127.

"new, emerging development in that understanding . . . simple, unquestionable, and inflexible dictate for nonintervention": Vucetich, Nelson, and Peterson, "Should Isle Royale Wolves Be Reintroduced?" 127.

"winking out": Cochrane, "Island Complications," 313.

37 "A thing is right when it tends to preserve the integrity": Vucetich, Nelson, and Peterson, "Discernment and Precaution," 337.

75 "You'd think if you had such dietary": Michigan Technological University, "Poo's clues."

84 "I HESITATE to write": Longstreth, *Lake Superior Country*, 313–14.

All other quotations were taken from interviews conducted by the author on Isle Royale during the week of June 6–14, 2019, or from follow-up email correspondence.

BIBLIOGRAPHY

Allen, Durward Leon. *Wolves of Minong: Isle Royale's Wild Community*. Ann Arbor: University of Michigan Press, 1983.

Cochrane, Timothy. "Island Complications: Should We Retain Wolves on Isle Royale?" *George Wright Forum* 30, no. 3 (2013): 313–25.

Cochrane, Timothy. *Minong: The Good Place: Ojibwe and Isle Royale*. East Lansing: Michigan State University Press, 2009.

Cochrane, Timothy. "Rejoinder to 'Discernment and Precaution: A Response to Cochrane and Mech.'" *George Wright Forum* 31, no. 1 (2014): 94–95.

Hairston, N. G., F. E. Smith, and L. B. Slobodkin. "Community Structure, Population Control, and Competition." *American Naturalist* 94 (1960): 421–25. www.esf.edu/efb/parry/Insect%20Ecology%20Reading/Hairston_etal_1960.pdf.

Hoy, Sarah R., et al. "Negative Frequency-Dependent Foraging Behaviour in a Generalist Herbivore (*Alces alces*) and Its Stabilizing Influence on Food Web Dynamics." *Journal of Animal Ecology* 88, no. 9 (2019): 1291–1304. doi .org/10.1111/1365-2656.13031.

Longstreth, T. Morris. *Lake Superior Country*. New York: Century Company, 1924. archive.org/stream/in.ernet.dli.2015.169017/2015.169017.The-Lake-Superior-Country_djvu.txt.

Mech, L. David. "The Case for Watchful Waiting with Isle Royale's Wolf Population." *George Wright Forum* 30, no. 3 (2013): 326–32.

Michigan Technological University. "Poo's clues: Moose droppings indicate Isle Royale ecosystem health." ScienceDaily, August 13, 2019. www.sciencedaily.com/releases/2019/08/190813105439.htm.

Peterson, Carolyn C. *A View from the Wolf's Eye*. Houghton, MI: Isle Royale Natural History Association, 2008.

Peterson, Rolf O. "The Wolves and Moose of Isle Royale." Webinar hosted by Wolf Conservation Center, April 24, 2019.

Peterson, Rolf O. *The Wolves of Isle Royale: A Broken Balance*. Ann Arbor: University of Michigan Press, 2007.

Scarpino, Philip V. "Isle Royale National Park: Balancing Human and Natural History in a Maritime Park." *George Wright Forum* 28, no. 2 (2011): 182–98.

Vucetich, John A., Michael P. Nelson, and Rolf O. Peterson. "Discernment and Precaution: A Response to Cochrane and Mech." *George Wright Forum* 30, no. 3 (2013): 333–40.

Vucetich, John A., Michael P. Nelson, and Rolf O. Peterson. "Should Isle Royale Wolves Be Reintroduced? A Case Study on Wilderness Management in a Changing World." *George Wright Forum* 2, no. 1 (2012): 126–47.

Vucetich, John A., Rolf O. Peterson, and Carrie L. Schaefer. "The Effect of Prey and Predator Densities." *Ecology* 83, no. 11 (2002): 3003–13. www.isleroyalewolf.org/sites/default/files/tech_pubs_files/Vucetichetal2002.pdf.

ACKNOWLEDGMENTS

MY THANKS RUN AS DEEP as the waters of Lake Superior. First, to the professor who introduced me to Isle Royale's predator/prey study—Dr. Warren Balgooyan, a wonderful adjunct professor who taught four enthusiastic young women, and to Marymount College, Tarrytown, for hiring someone to teach a class for me when I refused to graduate without taking ecology. It was a gift I open every day.

Second, my thanks pour out to author pals Carrie Pearson and Leslie Helakoski, who shared their Upper Penninsual with me and provided me with their contacts, who ignited my research. They are friends beyond compare.

Third, I thank my husband, Dean, who shared this research experience with me, carried Mo's equipment, captained our boat on the Great Lake, and hiked miles with us—my forever partner on and off the trail.

My unending gratitude extends to the researchers on Isle Royale, my fabulous agent-friend Jennifer Laughran, my crit buds Lois Huey and Anita Sanchez, my editor Erica Zappy for acquiring this, and the amazing team at Houghton Mifflin, including Catherine Onder, Megan Gendell, Cara Llewellyn, and editors Lily Kessinger and Elizabeth Agyemang. This was a fun one, and you all made it a fantastic experience. Thank you!

Dean Castaldo looking out at Lake Superior from an Isle Royale hike.

Nancy with Rolf and Candy Peterson at Bangsund Cabin.

Morgan photographing on Isle Royale in the early morning.

INDEX

SCIENTISTS IN THE FIELD

THE BIG ONE
GEOLOGY
SCIENTISTS IN THE FIELD
The Cascadia Earthquakes and the Science of Saving Lives
BY ELIZABETH RUSCH

CONDOR COMEBACK
CONSERVATION
SCIENTISTS IN THE FIELD
Words by SY MONTGOMERY
Photographs by TIANNE STROMBECK

ECLIPSE CHASER
Science in the Moon's Shadow
THE SUN
SCIENTISTS IN THE FIELD
by ILIMA LOOMIS
with photographs by AMANDA COWAN

SAVING THE TASMANIAN DEVIL
How Science is Helping the World's Largest Marsupial Carnivore Survive
CONSERVATION
SCIENTISTS IN THE FIELD
Dorothy Hinshaw Patent

THE TORNADO SCIENTIST
Seeing Inside Severe Storms
WEATHER
SCIENTISTS IN THE FIELD
MARY KAY CARSON
WITH PHOTOGRAPHS BY TOM UHLMAN

BACKYARD BEARS
Conservation, Habitat Changes, and the Rise of Urban Wildlife
CONSERVATION
SCIENTISTS IN THE FIELD
BY AMY CHERRIX

THE ORCA SCIENTISTS
PACIFIC NORTHWEST
SCIENTISTS IN THE FIELD
by Kim Perez Valice | With photographs by Andy Comins and Center for Whale Research

THE HYENA SCIENTIST
AFRICAN PLAINS
SCIENTISTS IN THE FIELD
written by Sy Montgomery photographs by Nic Bishop

IMPACT!
ASTEROIDS AND THE SCIENCE OF SAVING THE WORLD
ASTEROIDS
SCIENTISTS IN THE FIELD
Elizabeth Rusch
Photos by Karin Anderson

Where Science Meets Adventure

sciencemeetsadventure.com